Ten Essays on AI

NAVIGATING THE TRANSFORMATIVE
WORLD OF ARTIFICIAL INTELLIGENCE

Partha Majumdar

Copyright © 2024 Partha Majumdar

All rights reserved.

No part of this book may be reproduced, stored in a retrieval system, or transmitted in any form or by any means, electronic, mechanical, photocopying, recording, or otherwise, without express written permission of the author.

ISBN-13: 9798333525833

Cover design by Partha Majumdar.

Unless explicitly stated, all images are created by the author or licensed from Adobe.

B

Dedicated to

Prof. (Dr.) Deepak Subramaniam.

Your lectures increased my curiosity to learn more about AI.

Preface

In the rapidly evolving world of artificial intelligence (AI), understanding its core concepts and practical applications is paramount for professionals across industries. "Ten Essays on AI" is designed to bridge the gap between theoretical knowledge and real-world application, providing readers with a comprehensive overview of AI's transformative potential. This collection of essays delves into various facets of AI, from data-analytic thinking and data quality to the intricacies of data mining processes and the profound impact of AI on business operations.

Each chapter is meticulously crafted to offer insights into specific areas of AI, ensuring that readers can grasp both the foundational theories and the latest advancements. Whether you are a data scientist, a business leader, or simply an AI enthusiast, this book aims to enhance your understanding and appreciation of AI's role in shaping our future.

I have drawn from years of research, industry experience, and academic insights to compile these essays. This book informs and inspires readers to explore the vast possibilities AI offers. I invite you to embark on this journey through the realms of artificial intelligence and discover how it is transforming the world as we know it.

Partha Majumdar

d

e

Table of Contents

PREFACE .... **B**

TRANSFORMATIVE DATA-ANALYTIC THINKING: AN OVERVIEW **1**

    ABSTRACT 1
    INTRODUCTION 2
    THE IMPORTANCE OF DATA-ANALYTIC THINKING 2
    DATA-DRIVEN DECISION-MAKING 3
    TYPES OF DATA AND THEIR SIGNIFICANCE 4
    FROM SMALL DATA TO BIG DATA 5
    LEARNING FROM DATA 6
    ANALYTICAL THINKING MODELS 7
    CONCLUSION 8
    REFERENCES 9
    ADDITIONAL READING MATERIAL 9

ENSURING DATA QUALITY: A COMPREHENSIVE GUIDE TO DATA PREPARATION FOR EFFECTIVE MODEL BUILDING **11**

    ABSTRACT 11
    INTRODUCTION 12
    DATA CLEANING 12
    DATA TRANSFORMATION 13
    FEATURE SELECTION 15
    CONCLUSION 16
    ADDITIONAL READING MATERIAL 17

UNDERSTANDING THE GENERIC DATA MINING PROCESS: A COMPREHENSIVE GUIDE **19**

f

ABSTRACT	19
INTRODUCTION	20
THE CRISP-DM FRAMEWORK	20
THE GENERIC DATA MINING PROCESS	25
ADVANCED MODELLING TECHNIQUES	27
MODEL EVALUATION METRICS	28
CONCLUSION	28
REFERENCES	29
ADDITIONAL READING MATERIAL	30

LEVERAGING DATA-DRIVEN DECISION-MAKING FOR BUSINESS SUCCESS 31

ABSTRACT	31
INTRODUCTION	32
DATA-DRIVEN DECISION-MAKING: AN OVERVIEW	32
DECISION-DRIVEN DATA ANALYTICS	33
TYPES OF DATA ANALYTICS	34
UNDERSTANDING DATA TYPES	36
DATA CATEGORIES FOR BUSINESS INTELLIGENCE	37
THE DATA CYCLE	38
FROM SMALL DATA TO BIG DATA	39
LEVELS OF DATA	39
LEARNING FROM DATA	40
CONCLUSION	41
REFERENCES	42
ADDITIONAL READING MATERIAL	43

FROM SMALL DATA TO BIG DATA 45

ABSTRACT	45
INTRODUCTION	46
THE 4 VS OF DATA	46

g

    Value 51
    Practical Example 52
    Data Warehouses to Data Lakes 53
    Case Studies 53
    Conclusion 55
    References 56
    Additional Reading 58

THE EVOLUTION AND IMPACT OF ARTIFICIAL INTELLIGENCE: FROM TURING TO GENERATIVE AI 59

    Abstract 59
    Introduction 60
    The Turing Test 60
    CAPTCHA and AI Evolution 61
    Promises and Perils of AI 62
    Applications of AI 62
    Historical Milestones in AI 63
    Classifications of AI 64
    The Impact on Job Roles 65
    Conclusion 65
    References 66
    Additional Reading 69

CRAFTING EFFECTIVE AI STRATEGIES: FROM OBJECTIVES TO IMPLEMENTATION 71

    Abstract 71
    Introduction 72
    Defining AI Strategy Objectives and Goals 72
    Assessing Organisational Readiness for AI Adoption
    76

h

ALIGNING AI STRATEGY WITH BUSINESS GOALS AND VISION 79
DEVELOPING A ROADMAP FOR AI IMPLEMENTATION 83
BUILDING AI INFRASTRUCTURE AND CAPABILITIES 87
ESTABLISHING AI GOVERNANCE AND COMPLIANCE FRAMEWORKS 93
IDENTIFYING KEY STAKEHOLDERS AND ROLES IN AI STRATEGY EXECUTION 97
MEASURING AND EVALUATING THE SUCCESS OF AI STRATEGY IMPLEMENTATION 101
ITERATIVE IMPROVEMENT AND ADAPTATION OF AI STRATEGY 105
CONCLUSION 109
REFERENCES 110
ADDITIONAL READING 117

TRANSFORMING BUSINESS OPERATIONS WITH AI INTEGRATION...119

ABSTRACT 119
INTRODUCTION 120
THE IMPORTANCE OF DATA 120
ENHANCING OPERATIONAL EFFICIENCY 121
PERSONALISING CUSTOMER EXPERIENCES 122
RISK MANAGEMENT AND FRAUD DETECTION 123
CHALLENGES IN AI INTEGRATION 123
CASE STUDIES 124
BEST PRACTICES FOR AI INTEGRATION 126
ENSURING DATA SECURITY AND PRIVACY 129
FUTURE TRENDS IN AI INTEGRATION 133
CONCLUSION 136
REFERENCES 137

Additional Reading 138

THE TRANSFORMATIVE IMPACT OF GENERATIVE AI ON MODERN BUSINESS OPERATIONS 139

Abstract 139
Introduction 140
Exploring Generative AI and Its Potential 141
Ethical and Practical Challenges 142
Harnessing the Potential of Generative AI 142
Case Studies 143
Integrating Generative AI into Leadership and Management 144
Decision-Making in the Age of Generative AI 145
Challenges in Integrating Generative AI 146
Enhancing Creativity and Innovation 146
Ethical and Societal Implications 147
Conclusion 147
References 148
Additional Reading 150

CULTIVATING AN AI-READY ORGANIZATIONAL CULTURE 151

Abstract 151
Introduction 151
Commitment to Learning and Adaptability 152
Promoting Teamwork and Collaboration 153
Leadership Support and Commitment 154
Transparency and Ethical Considerations 156
Fostering a Data-Driven Decision-Making Culture 157
Recognising and Celebrating AI Successes 158

j

CONCLUSION 159
REFERENCES 160
ADDITIONAL READING 161

ABOUT THE AUTHOR... **I**

BOOKS BY THE AUTHOR.. III

m

Transformative Data-Analytic Thinking: An Overview

Abstract

In the modern business landscape, data is often heralded as the new "oil," driving transformative changes across industries through digitisation and digitalisation. This article delves into the concepts and applications of data-analytic thinking, data-driven decision-making, various data types, the evolution from small to big data, and the essential role of data science. By exploring these elements, we aim to provide a comprehensive understanding of how businesses can leverage data to enhance decision-making, foster innovation, and sustain growth.

Introduction

Data is one of the most essential commodities in today's world, often compared to oil in terms of its value and impact. The process of digitisation has enabled the transformation of information into digital formats, facilitating storage, processing, and electronic transmission. As digital data becomes more prevalent, companies are embracing digitalisation, integrating digital technologies to transform business processes, improve efficiency, and enhance customer experiences. This article explores how businesses can cultivate an AI-ready organisational culture by leveraging data-analytic thinking and various data-mining processes to unlock value and drive growth.

The Importance of Data-Analytic Thinking

Data-analytic thinking is a philosophy that integrates data, analytics, and critical thinking to improve decision-making processes. Unlike traditional decision-making, which relies on intuition and experience, data-analytic thinking emphasises the systematic analysis of data to derive actionable insights. This approach is essential in a rapidly evolving digital business era, where data is collected at an unprecedented pace, necessitating efficient and effective utilisation.

To illustrate, consider Amazon's transformation from an online bookseller to a leading cloud service provider. By capitalising on digital technologies, Amazon has continuously innovated and expanded its scope, demonstrating the power of data-analytic thinking in driving business transformation.

Data-Driven Decision-Making

Decision-making in business involves evaluating multiple options based on various criteria to make informed choices. Data-driven decision-making leverages data analytics to uncover insights, identify patterns, and support evidence-based decisions. This approach ensures that decisions are grounded in objective data rather than solely on intuition or subjective judgment.

For example, a retail company deciding which products to stock for the upcoming season can analyse past sales data, market trends, and customer preferences to make data-driven decisions, optimising inventory and maximising sales.

Types of Data and Their Significance

Understanding the different types of data is crucial for effective data analytics. Data can be classified into structured, semi-structured, and unstructured categories, each with unique characteristics and implications for analysis.

- **Structured Data**: Organized in a specific format, such as tables with rows

and columns, making it easy to analyse. Examples include databases and spreadsheets.
- **Semi-Structured Data**: Contains tags or markers to separate data elements, providing more flexibility than structured data. Examples include XML and JSON files.
- **Unstructured Data**: Does not follow a specific format, including social media posts, emails, and multimedia content. Requires extensive preprocessing for analysis.

The distinction between these data types is essential for selecting appropriate analytical techniques and tools.

From Small Data to Big Data

The transition from small data to big data has revolutionised data processing and analysis.

Small data refers to manageable datasets, while big data encompasses vast, complex datasets that require advanced tools for processing. Big data's volume, variety, and velocity present unique challenges and opportunities for businesses.

For instance, big data allows companies to analyse social media interactions, sensor data, and real-time transactions to gain deeper insights and make more informed decisions. This transition has also led to the shift from traditional data warehouses to more flexible data lakes capable of storing diverse and unstructured data.

Learning from Data

Both humans and machines learn from data to adapt and make dynamic decisions. Machine learning, a subset of data science, involves using algorithms to identify patterns and make predictions. There are four main types of machine learning:

- **Supervised Learning**: Learning from labelled data to make predictions.
- **Unsupervised Learning**: Identifying patterns in unlabelled data.
- **Semi-supervised learning** combines a small amount of labelled data with a large amount of unlabelled data.
- **Reinforcement Learning**: Learning through interaction with the environment, receiving rewards or punishments based on actions.

These learning methods enable businesses to enhance processes and decision-making, driving competitive advantages.

Analytical Thinking Models

Analytical thinking models are essential for problem-solving in business. These models involve identifying problems, collecting relevant data, and using mathematical or computational techniques to derive solutions.

The quality of the model directly impacts the accuracy and reliability of the solutions.

For example, financial forecasting can use simple linear regression models for approximate solutions or complex machine learning models for precise predictions. Understanding and applying the appropriate models is crucial for practical data analysis and decision-making.

Conclusion

Data-analytic thinking is a powerful tool that enables businesses to harness the power of data for strategic decision-making. By understanding data science, learning from data, and applying analytical thinking models, managers can drive success in their organisations. Embracing a data-driven culture, fostering collaboration, and ensuring ethical and transparent AI practices are essential steps in leveraging data for growth and innovation.

References

- Davenport, T. H., & Harris, J. G. (2007). *Competing on Analytics: The New Science of Winning*. Harvard Business Review Press.
- Hand, D. J. (2007). *Principles of Data Mining*. MIT Press.
- Mayer-Schönberger, V., & Cukier, K. (2013). *Big Data: A Revolution That Will Transform How We Live, Work, and Think*. Houghton Mifflin Harcourt.
- Provost, F., & Fawcett, T. (2013). *Data Science for Business: What You Need to Know about Data Mining and Data-Analytic Thinking*. O'Reilly Media.

Additional Reading Material

- Berson, A., Smith, S. J., & Thearling, K. (2002). *Building Data Mining Applications for CRM*. McGraw-Hill.
- McKinsey Global Institute. (2011). *Big data: The next frontier for innovation,*

competition, and productivity. McKinsey & Company.
- Witten, I. H., Frank, E., & Hall, M. A. (2011). *Data Mining: Practical Machine Learning Tools and Techniques*. Morgan Kaufmann.

Ensuring Data Quality: A Comprehensive Guide to Data Preparation for Effective Model Building

Abstract

Data preparation is a critical step in the data mining and machine learning process, consuming a significant portion of the project's time and effort. This article delves into the various aspects of data preparation, including data cleaning, transformation, and feature selection, highlighting their importance in building reliable and accurate models. By understanding these processes, businesses and data scientists can ensure that their models are built on high-quality data, leading to better decision-making and insights.

Introduction

In the realm of data science, the adage "garbage in, garbage out" underscores the importance of high-quality data. William S. Cleveland and other pioneers in data science have emphasised that data preparation efforts constitute about 60% of the total time required for completing a data mining project. This article explores the critical steps in data preparation, including data cleaning, transformation, and feature selection, and their significance in building reliable models.

Data Cleaning

Data cleaning involves identifying and rectifying errors, inconsistencies, and missing values in the raw data collected from various sources such as sensors, computer programs, manual entry, IoT devices, social media, and cloud databases. Raw data can often be incomplete, noisy, or contain obsolete fields. Addressing these issues is crucial for accurate analysis and modelling.

- **Handling Missing Values**: Missing data can be managed using methods like mean, mode, median imputation, k-nearest neighbours, and advanced techniques like Multiple Imputation by Chained Equations (MICE). The choice of method depends on the nature and extent of the missing data.
- **Detecting and Handling Outliers**: Outliers, which are extreme values significantly different from the rest of the data, can skew analysis and model performance. Techniques such as box plots, scatter plots, and advanced methods like Isolation Forest and DBSCAN can be used to identify and handle outliers effectively.

Data Transformation

Data transformation involves converting data into a suitable format for modelling while preserving its original meaning. This process ensures consistency and compatibility with various machine-learning algorithms.

- **Data Scaling**: Data scaling is essential for normalising or standardising the range of data values, making them suitable for algorithms sensitive to variable scales. Popular scaling methods include normalisation (adjusting data to a specific range) and standardisation (transforming data to have a mean of zero and a standard deviation of one).
- **Data Encoding**: Converting categorical data into numerical formats is crucial for machine learning models that require numerical inputs. Techniques like ordinal encoding (for ordered categories) and one-hot encoding (for nominal categories) are commonly used.
- **Transforming Numerical Data to Categorical Data**: In some cases, converting continuous numerical data into discrete categories can be beneficial. For example, age can be categorised into groups such as 'non-adult', 'adult', and 'old age' to facilitate specific analyses.

Feature Selection

Feature selection is the process of identifying and retaining the most relevant features while eliminating redundant or irrelevant ones. This step simplifies the model, improves performance, and enhances interpretability.

- **Data Transformation by Compression**: Combining related features to create a single, more informative feature can reduce the number of variables. For instance, Body Mass Index (BMI) combines weight and height into one feature, often performing better than using weight and height separately.
- **Dimensionality Reduction**: Techniques like Principal Component Analysis (PCA) reduce the number of features by transforming them into a new set of variables called principal components. These components retain most of the information from the original features, making the dataset more manageable and informative.

- **Advanced Feature Selection Methods**: Methods like Recursive Feature Elimination (RFE) and Lasso Regression are used to reduce the number of features systematically. RFE recursively removes the least important features, while Lasso Regression adds a penalty for the number of features used, effectively eliminating those with minimal impact.

Conclusion

Proper data preparation is foundational to building effective and efficient machine learning models. By cleaning, transforming, and selecting the right features, data scientists can ensure that their models are built on high-quality data, leading to more accurate and reliable insights. Understanding and applying these techniques is crucial for achieving successful outcomes in data-driven projects.

Additional Reading Material

- Breiman, L. (2001). *Random Forests*. Machine Learning.
- Cleveland, W. S. (1999). *Data mining and data science*.
- Domingos, P. (2015). *The Master Algorithm: How the Quest for the Ultimate Learning Machine Will Remake Our World*.
- Friedman, J., Hastie, T., & Tibshirani, R. (2010). *Regularization Paths for Generalized Linear Models via Coordinate Descent*.
- Géron, A. (2019). *Hands-On Machine Learning with Scikit-Learn, Keras, and TensorFlow*.
- Han, J., Pei, J., & Kamber, M. (2011). *Data Mining: Concepts and Techniques*.
- Hastie, T., Tibshirani, R., & Friedman, J. (2009). *The Elements of Statistical Learning*.
- Kuhn, M., & Johnson, K. (2013). *Applied Predictive Modeling*.

- Little, R. J. A., & Rubin, D. B. (2002). *Statistical Analysis with Missing Data.*
- Provost, F., & Fawcett, T. (2013). *Data Science for Business: What You Need to Know About Data Mining and Data-Analytic Thinking.*

Understanding the Generic Data Mining Process: A Comprehensive Guide

Abstract

The generic data mining process is a structured approach to extracting valuable insights from vast amounts of data. This article delves into the various stages of the data mining process, derived from the CRISP-DM (Cross Industry Standard Process for Data Mining) framework, emphasising the importance of data preparation, business understanding, and model building. By understanding and applying these stages, businesses can effectively solve complex problems and make informed decisions.

Introduction

Data mining is a critical component of the data science process, aimed at discovering patterns and insights from large datasets. The most widely adopted framework for data mining is the CRISP-DM process, which stands for Cross Industry Standard Process for Data Mining. This article explores the CRISP-DM framework and its adaptation in the generic data mining process, highlighting the key stages and their importance in building reliable models and making data-driven decisions.

The CRISP-DM Framework

CRISP-DM is a robust framework that outlines the data mining process in six stages: business understanding, data understanding, data preparation, modelling, evaluation, and deployment. It provides a structured approach to data mining, ensuring that each step is meticulously executed to achieve accurate and actionable insights (Chapman et al., 2000; Wirth & Hipp, 2000).

1. Business Understanding

- This initial stage focuses on understanding the business context and objectives. It involves defining the problem to be solved and determining how data mining can address it. Questions such as "What problems are we going to solve?" and "How does it fit in the business context?" are crucial at this stage (Wirth & Hipp, 2000).
- Business understanding is combined with data understanding in the generic data mining process, forming the foundation for the subsequent steps. This combined block, known as prior knowledge, helps in identifying the data requirements and formulating a well-defined problem statement (Wirth & Hipp, 2000).

2. **Data Understanding**
    - Data understanding involves exploring the data to identify its characteristics and assess its quality. This stage includes data collection, initial data analysis, and identifying any data issues, such as missing values or outliers (Chapman et al., 2000).
    - The data understanding phase goes hand in hand with business understanding, ensuring that the data collected aligns with the business objectives and is suitable for analysis (Wirth & Hipp, 2000).

3. **Data Preparation**
    - Data preparation is the most time-consuming part of the data mining process. It involves cleaning the data, handling missing values, removing outliers, and transforming the data into a suitable format for modelling (Chapman et al., 2000; Hastie, Tibshirani, & Friedman, 2009).

- This stage ensures that the data is of high quality and ready for analysis, forming the basis for building accurate models.

4. Modelling
- Modelling is the core of the data mining process, where algorithms are applied to the prepared data to build predictive or descriptive models. This stage involves selecting the appropriate modelling techniques, training the models, and tuning their parameters to achieve the best performance (Chapman et al., 2000; Hastie et al., 2009).
- Different types of data, such as training, validation, and test data, are used in this stage to ensure that the model is robust and performs well on unseen data.

5. Evaluation
- The evaluation stage assesses the performance of the models built in the previous stage. It involves testing the models on validation and test datasets to ensure they generalise well to new data and meet the business objectives (Chapman et al., 2000; Hastie et al., 2009).
- This stage is crucial for validating the model's accuracy and effectiveness before deploying it in a production environment.

6. Deployment
- Deployment involves integrating the model into the business processes and making it operational. This stage ensures that the model is production-ready, providing valuable insights and supporting decision-making in real time (Chapman et al., 2000).
- Continuous monitoring and re-evaluation are essential to keep the

model relevant and up-to-date with changing business needs and data dynamics (Wirth & Hipp, 2000).

The Generic Data Mining Process

The generic data mining process reorganises the CRISP-DM framework into a more streamlined approach. The initial two blocks, business understanding and data understanding, are combined into a single block that provides prior knowledge. This reorganisation emphasises the importance of having a clear understanding of the business and data requirements from the outset (Wirth & Hipp, 2000).

1. Prior Knowledge

This combined block sets the stage for the data mining process by providing a comprehensive understanding of the business context and data requirements. It ensures that the problem statement is well-defined and that the data collected is relevant and suitable for analysis (Chapman et al., 2000).

2. Data Preparation

As highlighted earlier, data preparation is crucial for building reliable models. This stage involves cleaning, transforming, and preparing the data for analysis, ensuring its quality and suitability for modelling (Hastie et al., 2009).

3. Modelling

The modelling stage in the generic data mining process involves building and testing models using the prepared data. Different algorithms and techniques are applied to find the best model that addresses the business problem effectively (Breiman, 2001; Friedman, 2001).

4. **Application and Knowledge Acquisition**

Once the model is built and tested, it needs to be deployed in a production environment. This stage ensures that the model is production-ready and integrated with other business processes. The knowledge acquired from the data mining process adds to the organisation's knowledge base, enhancing its ability to make informed decisions (Chapman et al., 2000; Wirth & Hipp, 2000).

Advanced Modelling Techniques

Advanced modelling techniques, such as ensemble methods like Random Forest and Gradient Boosting, offer more accurate and stable predictions. These techniques build multiple models and combine their predictions to improve performance and robustness (Breiman, 2001; Friedman, 2001). For instance, Random Forest builds various decision trees and merges them for more accurate predictions, while Gradient Boosting sequentially builds models to correct errors made by previous ones.

Model Evaluation Metrics

Different model evaluation metrics, such as accuracy, precision, recall, F1 score, and ROC-AUC, are essential for comprehensively assessing model performance. These metrics provide insights into the model's behaviour and help in interpreting the results effectively (Hastie et al., 2009).

Conclusion

The generic data mining process, derived from the CRISP-DM framework, provides a structured and practical approach to extracting valuable insights from data. By understanding and applying the stages of business understanding, data preparation, modelling, and deployment, businesses can solve complex problems and make informed decisions. Continuous monitoring and re-evaluation ensure that models remain relevant and practical, contributing to the organisation's knowledge base and overall success.

References

- Breiman, L. (2001). *Random forests*. Machine Learning, 45(1), 5-32.
- Chapman, P., Clinton, J., Kerber, R., Khabaza, T., Reinartz, T., Shearer, C., & Wirth, R. (2000). *CRISP-DM 1.0: Step-by-step data mining guide*.
- Friedman, J. H. (2001). *Greedy function approximation: A gradient boosting machine*. Annals of Statistics, 29(5), 1189-1232.
- Hastie, T., Tibshirani, R., & Friedman, J. (2009). *The Elements of Statistical Learning: Data Mining, Inference, and Prediction*. Springer.
- Wirth, R., & Hipp, J. (2000). *CRISP-DM: Towards a standard process model for data mining*.

Additional Reading Material

- Domingos, P. (2015). *The Master Algorithm: How the Quest for the Ultimate Learning Machine Will Remake Our World*. Basic Books.
- Géron, A. (2019). *Hands-On Machine Learning with Scikit-Learn, Keras, and TensorFlow*. O'Reilly Media.
- Han, J., Pei, J., & Kamber, M. (2011). *Data Mining: Concepts and Techniques*. Morgan Kaufmann.
- Kuhn, M., & Johnson, K. (2013). *Applied Predictive Modeling*. Springer.
- Provost, F., & Fawcett, T. (2013). *Data Science for Business: What You Need to Know About Data Mining and Data-Analytic Thinking*. O'Reilly Media.

Leveraging Data-Driven Decision-Making for Business Success

Abstract

Data-driven decision-making is a cornerstone of modern business strategy. By leveraging data analytics, companies can enhance decision-making processes, optimise operations, and drive better business outcomes. This article delves into the fundamentals of data-driven decision-making, comparing it with decision-driven data analytics, and explores various types of data and analytics methods. It emphasises the importance of integrating intuition with data insights and discusses the significance of understanding data types, categories, and the data cycle in business intelligence and analytics.

Introduction

In today's dynamic business environment, the ability to make informed decisions is critical. Data-driven decision-making, which involves using data to guide decisions, plays a pivotal role in improving business outcomes. This approach ensures that decisions are grounded in objective data rather than solely on intuition or subjective judgment. This article explores the principles of data-driven decision-making, compares it with decision-driven data analytics, and discusses the various types and categories of data essential for practical business intelligence.

Data-Driven Decision-Making: An Overview

Data-driven decision-making involves collecting, analysing, and leveraging data to inform decisions. This approach helps businesses uncover insights, identify patterns, and support evidence-based decision-making. The process begins with data collection from various sources, followed by data analysis using techniques such as statistical analysis, data mining, and machine learning. The insights gained from this analysis guide informed decisions, ensuring accuracy and effectiveness.

For instance, a retail company might analyse past sales data, market trends, and customer preferences to decide which products to stock for the upcoming season. This data-driven approach helps optimise inventory and maximise sales, reducing the risk of stockouts or overstocking (Davenport & Harris, 2007).

Decision-Driven Data Analytics

Contrasting with data-driven decision-making, decision-driven data analytics starts with a specific decision or goal and then collects and analyses relevant data to support that decision. This approach ensures that data collection and analysis are focused and aligned with the predefined objective. For example, a hotel chain aiming to improve customer satisfaction might start by defining the goal of increasing positive reviews. They would then collect and analyse data on customer feedback to implement improvements based on the insights gained (Provost & Fawcett, 2013).

Types of Data Analytics

Data analytics can be broadly categorised into four types: descriptive, diagnostic, predictive, and prescriptive analytics.

1. **Descriptive Analytics**: This involves techniques that summarise historical data to understand what has happened in the past. It includes data queries, reports, and data visualisation charts like dashboards. Descriptive analytics helps answer questions such as, "Is there an increase in customers this month?" (Shmueli et al., 2010).
2. **Diagnostic Analytics**: This type focuses on understanding why

something happened. It involves analysing data to identify the causes of past events. For example, diagnostic analytics can help determine if a marketing campaign increased sales and why it was effective (Davenport & Harris, 2007).
3. **Predictive Analytics**: Predictive analytics uses models constructed from past data to forecast future events. It helps predict outcomes such as future sales, customer behaviour, and market trends. Techniques include regression and classification algorithms (Chen et al., 2012).
4. **Prescriptive Analytics**: This involves recommending actions to achieve desired outcomes. It uses optimisation models to prescribe the best course of action from available options. For example, prescriptive analytics can optimise supply chain logistics to minimise costs (Davenport & Harris, 2007).

Understanding Data Types

Effective data analytics requires understanding the different types of data: structured, semi-structured, and unstructured.

- **Structured Data**: Organized in a specific format, such as tables with rows and columns, structured data is accessible to analyse. Examples include databases and spreadsheets (Provost & Fawcett, 2013).
- **Semi-Structured Data**: Contains tags or markers to separate data elements but does not conform to a rigid structure. Examples include XML and JSON files (Han et al., 2011).
- **Unstructured Data**: Lacks a predefined format and includes free-form data such as social media posts, emails, and multimedia content (Chen et al., 2012).

Data Categories for Business Intelligence

Data can be categorised into primary and secondary data. Primary data is collected directly from the source through surveys, feedback, and opinion polls. Secondary data is gathered from existing sources such as census data, point-of-sales data, and business processes.

- **Behavioural Data**: Automatically collected when customers interact with systems, capturing actual actions taken by customers. For example, purchase history from an e-commerce site (Provost & Fawcett, 2013).
- **Attitudinal Data**: Relates to customer opinions and feelings gathered through surveys and feedback forms. It helps understand customer preferences and improve offerings (Shmueli et al., 2010).
- **Demographic Data**: Includes attributes like age, gender, education, and marital status. It helps segment

customers and tailor marketing strategies (Davenport & Harris, 2007).

The Data Cycle

The data cycle, or data pipeline, encompasses a series of processes that enable the collection, processing, and analysis of data. It involves data acquisition, preprocessing, analysis, and operationalisation. Data engineers, data scientists, developers, and business users play crucial roles in this cycle, transforming raw data into actionable insights.

For example, data engineers collect and preprocess data, data scientists develop analytical models, developers create user-friendly interfaces, and business users leverage insights for decision-making (Han et al., 2011).

From Small Data to Big Data

The transition from small data to big data has revolutionised data analytics. Small data refers to manageable datasets that can be processed with traditional tools. In contrast, big data involves large, diverse, and rapidly generated datasets requiring advanced tools and techniques for analysis.

Big data enables businesses to gain deeper insights and make more informed decisions. For instance, an e-commerce platform can use big data analytics to personalise user experiences, optimise pricing strategies, and forecast demand (Chen et al., 2012).

Levels of Data

Data can be classified into four levels: nominal, ordinal, interval, and ratio.

- **Nominal Data**: Consists of categories without any inherent order, such as

gender or types of products (Shmueli et al., 2010).
- **Ordinal Data**: Provides a rank order among items but does not quantify the difference between them (Davenport & Harris, 2007).
- **Interval Data**: Quantitative data allows for the comparison of differences between data points but lacks an actual zero point (Provost & Fawcett, 2013).
- **Ratio Data**: Has all the properties of interval data with a meaningful zero point, allowing for a full range of mathematical operations (Han et al., 2011).

Understanding these levels is crucial for selecting appropriate statistical methods for analysis.

Learning from Data

Machines can learn from data through supervised, unsupervised, semi-supervised, and reinforcement learning.

- **Supervised Learning**: Uses labelled data to train models to make predictions (Shmueli et al., 2010).
- **Unsupervised Learning**: Identifies patterns in unlabelled data (Provost & Fawcett, 2013).
- **Semi-supervised learning**: Combines a small amount of labelled data with a large amount of unlabelled data (Davenport & Harris, 2007).
- **Reinforcement Learning**: Learned through interaction with the environment and receiving feedback (Han et al., 2011).

Conclusion

Data-driven decision-making and decision-driven data analytics are essential for modern businesses. By understanding and leveraging different types of data and analytics methods, companies can make informed decisions, optimise operations, and gain competitive advantages. Integrating data insights with intuition and logical analysis helps businesses

navigate complexities and achieve better outcomes.

References

- Chen, H., Chiang, R. H., & Storey, V. C. (2012). *Business intelligence and analytics: From big data to significant impact*. MIS Quarterly, 36(4), 1165-1188.
- Davenport, T. H., & Harris, J. G. (2007). *Competing on Analytics: The New Science of Winning*. Harvard Business Review Press.
- Han, J., Pei, J., & Kamber, M. (2011). Data Mining: Concepts and Techniques. Elsevier.
- Provost, F., & Fawcett, T. (2013). *Data Science for Business: What You Need to Know about Data Mining and Data-Analytic Thinking*. O'Reilly Media.
- Shmueli, G., Patel, N. R., & Bruce, P. C. (2010). *Data Mining for Business Intelligence: Concepts, Techniques, and*

Applications in Microsoft Office Excel with XLMiner. Wiley.

Additional Reading Material

- Han, J., Pei, J., & Kamber, M. (2011). *Data Mining: Concepts and Techniques.* Elsevier.
- Hastie, T., Tibshirani, R., & Friedman, J. (2009). *The Elements of Statistical Learning: Data Mining, Inference, and Prediction.* Springer.
- McKinney, W. (2012). *Python for Data Analysis: Data Wrangling with Pandas, NumPy, and IPython.* O'Reilly Media.
- Silver, N. (2012). *The Signal and the Noise: Why So Many Predictions Fail—but Some Don't.* Penguin Press.

From Small Data to Big Data

Abstract

The transition from small data to big data has been a significant trend in the data industry, gaining popularity since 2010. Big data refers to datasets that exceed the processing capabilities of traditional data systems due to their sheer volume, variety, and velocity. This article explores the distinctions between small data and big data, focusing on their volume, variety, velocity, veracity, and value. By examining these characteristics, the article highlights the evolution of data processing and the tools required to manage big data. Furthermore, it discusses the practical applications and implications for businesses and the shift from traditional data warehouses to modern data lakes.

Introduction

The terms small data and big data refer to the volume, variety, and complexity of the data being processed. The transition from small data to big data has been a significant trend in the industry, gaining popularity since 2010. Big data refers to datasets that are beyond the processing capabilities of traditional data processing systems due to their sheer volume, variety, and velocity (Russom, 2011). If you can process the data with your current resources, it remains small data. Once it surpasses those capabilities, it becomes big data.

The 4 Vs of Data

In the realm of data analytics, understanding the fundamental characteristics that define the nature and challenges of data is crucial. These characteristics, often referred to as the "4 Vs of Data," provide a framework for distinguishing between different types of data and the approaches needed to manage and analyse them effectively. The 4 Vs—Volume, Variety, Velocity, and Veracity—highlight the key differences between small data and big data, illustrating the complexities and opportunities each type presents.

Volume

Small data typically refers to datasets that are relatively small in quantity, often up to a few gigabytes or terabytes. These datasets can be easily managed and processed using traditional data processing tools like relational databases. Examples of small data include sales records for a small business or customer feedback from a single survey (Russom, 2011).

Big data, on the other hand, encompasses datasets that are several terabytes to petabytes in size and beyond. These datasets often require advanced tools and techniques for storage, processing, and analysis. Examples of big data include the vast amounts of data generated by social media platforms, IoT devices, and large-scale e-commerce transactions (Manyika et al., 2017).

Variety

The variety of data also distinguishes small data from big data. Small data is typically structured and of a single type, such as tabular data stored in relational databases. For instance, a company's sales data stored in an SQL database is an example of small, structured data (Russell & Norvig, 2016).

Big data, however, is characterised by its diverse formats. It includes structured data, semi-structured data (like XML and JSON files), and unstructured data (like text, images, audio, and video). For example, a social media platform generates vast amounts of unstructured data in the form of posts, comments, and multimedia content alongside structured data like user profiles and transaction logs (Gandomi & Haider, 2015).

Velocity

Another critical characteristic of big data is its velocity, which refers to the speed at which data is generated and processed. Small data typically arrives at a slower, more manageable pace, allowing for batch processing. For example, a monthly sales report generated at the end of each month exemplifies small data with low velocity (Russom, 2011).

Big data, in contrast, is often generated at high speeds and requires real-time or near-real-time processing. This high velocity is evident in data streams from financial markets, live social media feeds, and real-time sensor data from IoT devices. Processing this data demands robust systems capable of handling high-frequency data input and rapid processing (Manyika et al., 2017).

Veracity

Data veracity, or the uncertainty of data, is another crucial factor. Small data often has higher veracity because it is easier to validate and ensure its quality. For instance, data collected from a controlled experiment or a well-designed survey tends to have fewer inconsistencies and errors (Gandomi & Haider, 2015).

Big data, however, comes with significant uncertainty and requires rigorous validation. The sheer volume and variety of big data make it prone to inaccuracies and inconsistencies. For example, social media data can include a mix of genuine user-generated content and spam or irrelevant information, necessitating advanced techniques for data cleaning and validation (Mayer-Schönberger & Cukier, 2013).

Value

The value of data, in terms of its relevance and usefulness, also differs between small and big data. Small data is often more immediately valuable for business decision-making because it can be quickly processed and analysed. For instance, a company can analyse customer feedback from a small survey to improve its products or services (Davenport & Patil, 2012).

Big data, while potentially more valuable due to the extensive insights it can offer, requires sophisticated tools and techniques to extract meaningful information. This process often involves complex data mining and predictive analytics to uncover patterns and trends. For example, an e-commerce platform might use big data analytics to personalise user experiences, optimise pricing strategies, and forecast demand (Manyika et al., 2017).

Practical Example

Consider a retail company. Small data might include sales records from a single store, which can be analysed to understand local customer preferences and optimise inventory for that store. This analysis might involve simple statistical methods and can be completed relatively quickly (Russell & Norvig, 2016).

In contrast, big data for the same retail company might include sales records from all stores worldwide, along with customer reviews, social media interactions, and real-time inventory data. Analysing this big data requires advanced tools like Hadoop or Spark, machine learning algorithms, and real-time processing capabilities. The insights gained from this analysis can help the company optimise its global supply chain, personalise marketing campaigns, and predict future sales trends (Gandomi & Haider, 2015).

Data Warehouses to Data Lakes

The journey from small data to big data also involves transitioning from traditional data warehouses to modern data lakes. Data warehouses, while still in use, are becoming outdated due to their limitations in handling the diverse and unstructured nature of big data. Data lakes, on the other hand, offer more flexibility by storing both structured and unstructured data in its raw form, allowing for more comprehensive analysis and insights (Chen et al., 2014).

Case Studies

To fully appreciate the transformative power of big data, it is essential to examine real-world examples of how large organisations leverage vast datasets to drive business success. Case studies provide invaluable insights into the practical applications and benefits of big data analytics across different industries. By exploring these case studies, we can understand how companies use big data to enhance operations, improve customer experiences, and maintain a competitive edge in the market.

Case Study 1: Walmart

Walmart, one of the largest retail chains in the world, leverages big data to optimise its operations and enhance customer experiences. Walmart processes over 2.5 petabytes of data every hour, generated from transactions, social media, and sensors. This data is analysed in real-time to manage inventory, predict customer preferences, and personalise marketing efforts. By using big data analytics, Walmart can quickly respond to market changes, ensuring that popular products are in stock and reducing waste from overstocking (Manyika et al., 2017).

Case Study 2: Netflix

Netflix, the global streaming service, uses big data analytics to recommend content to its users. Netflix collects data on viewing habits, search queries, and even the time of day users watch content. This data is processed to create personalised recommendations, enhancing user experience and engagement. By analysing big data, Netflix can predict what shows or movies a user is likely to enjoy, leading to higher satisfaction and retention rates. The use of big data has been a critical factor in Netflix's success, allowing it to deliver a tailored viewing experience to millions of subscribers worldwide (Gandomi & Haider, 2015).

Conclusion

Understanding the differences between small data and big data is crucial for effective data analytics and decision-making. Small data is easier to manage and analyse but offers limited insights. Big data, while challenging to process, provides a wealth of information that can drive significant business value. By leveraging the right tools and techniques, businesses can harness the power of big data to gain deeper insights, make more informed decisions, and stay competitive in the rapidly evolving digital landscape (Manyika et al., 2017).

References

- Bostrom, N. (2014). *Superintelligence: Paths, Dangers, Strategies*. Oxford University Press.
- Brynjolfsson, E., & McAfee, A. (2014). *The Second Machine Age: Work, Progress, and Prosperity in a Time of Brilliant Technologies*. W. W. Norton & Company.
- Chen, M., Mao, S., & Liu, Y. (2014). *Big Data: A Survey. Mobile Networks and Applications*, 19(2), 171-209.
- Davenport, T. H., & Patil, D. J. (2012). *Data Scientist: The Sexiest Job of the 21st Century*. Harvard Business Review.

- Gandomi, A., & Haider, M. (2015). *Beyond the hype: Big data concepts, methods, and analytics*. International Journal of Information Management, 35(2), 137-144.
- Manyika, J., Chui, M., Miremadi, M., Bughin, J., George, K., Willmott, P., & Dewhurst, M. (2017). *A Future That Works: Automation, Employment, and Productivity*. McKinsey Global Institute.
- Mayer-Schönberger, V., & Cukier, K. (2013). *Big Data: A Revolution That Will Transform How We Live, Work, and Think*. John Murray.
- Russell, S., & Norvig, P. (2016). *Artificial Intelligence: A Modern Approach*. Pearson.
- Russom, P. (2011). *Big Data Analytics*. TDWI Best Practices Report, Fourth Quarter.

Additional Reading

- Bessen, J. (2019). *AI and Jobs: The Role of Demand*. NBER Working Paper Series.
- Tegmark, M. (2017). *Life 3.0: Being Human in the Age of Artificial Intelligence*. Knopf.

The Evolution and Impact of Artificial Intelligence: From Turing to Generative AI

Abstract

Artificial intelligence (AI) endeavours to replicate or simulate human intelligence in machines, enabling them to perform tasks typically requiring human cognition. While AI systems currently excel in specific, narrow applications, the future promises advancements toward general and superintelligence. This article explores the history, classifications, and evolving capabilities of AI, highlighting both its potential and ethical considerations. It also examines the impact of AI on job roles, the economy, and society, emphasising the need for continuous adaptation and ethical

management of this transformative technology.

Introduction

Artificial intelligence (AI) is a discipline that seeks to replicate or simulate human intelligence in machines, allowing them to perform tasks that typically require human cognitive abilities. Unlike natural intelligence exhibited by humans and animals, AI systems perform tasks using algorithms and data but do not learn and reason in the same way as humans. Currently, AI systems have very narrow capabilities, excelling at tasks but lacking the general adaptability of human intelligence (Russell & Norvig, 2016).

The Turing Test

Alan Turing was the first to ask, "Can machines think?" He developed the Turing test to evaluate a computer's capability to think like a human (Turing, 1950). The test involves a human interrogator communicating with both a machine and a human through a text interface without knowing which is which. The interrogator poses challenges to determine which entity is the machine and which is the human. Simple questions, such as spelling words quickly or answering logical puzzles, are used to discern human-like behaviour from machine responses. While the Turing test has been influential, it has limitations in identifying intelligent behaviour not exhibited by humans (Oppy & Dowe, 2011).

CAPTCHA and AI Evolution

CAPTCHA, which stands for Completely Automated Public Turing Test to Tell Computers and Humans Apart, is designed to distinguish between human and machine responses. It uses mechanisms to prevent machines from imitating humans, serving as a reverse Turing test (Von Ahn et al., 2003). Advanced applications of AI, such as Tesla's autopilot system, highlight the progress beyond simple CAPTCHA tests to complex real-world problem-solving (Tesla, 2021).

Promises and Perils of AI

AI systems process data without awareness or consciousness of human existence. From the algorithm's perspective, each person is merely a data point. The development of general AI remains uncertain and debated, with timelines for achieving it varying widely (Bostrom, 2014). AI is a tool that can be used for good or ill, depending on its deployment. Examples like OpenAI's GPT-4 showcase advanced capabilities, but ethical considerations such as copyright and misuse must be managed (OpenAI, 2023).

Applications of AI

AI has the potential to automate tasks and improve the quality of life by handling vast amounts of data efficiently. With advancements in cloud computing and data storage technologies, AI systems can now process and analyse enormous datasets in real time. Applications range from reading and summarising documents to detecting gunshots and aiding in medical diagnostics (Goodfellow et al., 2016). AI can also create art, music, and poetry and even navigate challenging environments with robots like Boston Dynamics' Spot (Boston Dynamics, 2021).

Historical Milestones in AI

The history of AI is marked by significant milestones, from the introduction of the first artificial neural network by McCulloch and Pitts in 1943 to the development of autonomous robots like Elmer and Elsie in 1948 (McCulloch & Pitts, 1943). Other notable advancements include the creation of the first chatbot, Eliza, in 1964, the development of the backpropagation algorithm in 1969, and the introduction of the intelligent robot Shakey in 1970 (Weizenbaum, 1966; Rumelhart et al., 1986; Nilsson, 1984). More recent milestones include IBM Watson's Jeopardy win in 2010, the release of Apple's Siri in 2011, and DeepMind's AlphaGo defeating a world champion in 2016 (Ferrucci et al., 2010; Silver et al., 2016).

Classifications of AI

AI can be classified into three types: Artificial Narrow Intelligence (ANI), Artificial General Intelligence (AGI), and Artificial Super Intelligence (ASI). ANI, or weak AI, excels at specific tasks but lacks general intelligence. AGI, or strong AI, aims to mimic human intelligence and solve any problem but remains theoretical and unachieved. ASI represents a hypothetical future where machines surpass human intelligence in all domains, posing significant ethical and practical challenges (Bostrom, 2014).

The Impact on Job Roles

Automation and AI are transforming job roles across industries. While AI can automate repetitive tasks, it also enables the automation of complex data analysis and decision-making. This transformation is gradual, with industries like finance and retail leading the way. New job roles are emerging in AI development, maintenance, and ethical management, requiring a dynamic and adaptable workforce (Brynjolfsson & McAfee, 2014). The development of a vast data industry supports AI applications, necessitating expertise in data extraction, management, and security (Manyika et al., 2017).

Conclusion

AI has the potential to revolutionise various aspects of life, from automating mundane tasks to solving complex global challenges. However, its development comes with significant ethical and practical considerations.

As AI continues to evolve, it is crucial to ensure its fair and secure use while also preparing the workforce for new roles and responsibilities. Understanding and leveraging AI will be vital to staying competitive and innovative in the digital age (West, 2018).

References

- Boston Dynamics. (2021). *Spot*. Retrieved from https://www.bostondynamics.com/spot
- Bostrom, N. (2014). *Superintelligence: Paths, Dangers, Strategies*. Oxford University Press.
- Brynjolfsson, E., & McAfee, A. (2014). *The Second Machine Age: Work, Progress, and Prosperity in a Time of Brilliant Technologies*. W. W. Norton & Company.
- Ferrucci, D., Levas, A., Bagchi, S., Gondek, D., & Mueller, E. T. (2010). Building Watson: An overview of the DeepQA project. *AI magazine, 31*(3), 59-79.

- Goodfellow, I., Bengio, Y., & Courville, A. (2016). *Deep Learning*. MIT Press.
- Manyika, J., Chui, M., Miremadi, M., Bughin, J., George, K., Willmott, P., & Dewhurst, M. (2017). *A Future That Works: Automation, Employment, and Productivity*. McKinsey Global Institute.
- McCulloch, W. S., & Pitts, W. (1943). A logical calculus of the ideas immanent in nervous activity. *The bulletin of mathematical biophysics, 5*(4), 115-133.
- Nilsson, N. J. (1984). Shakey the robot. *SRI International*.
- OpenAI. (2023). *GPT-4 Technical Report*. Retrieved from https://www.openai.com/research/
- Oppy, G., & Dowe, D. (2011). The Turing Test. In Zalta, E. N. (Ed.), *The Stanford Encyclopedia of Philosophy*.
- Rumelhart, D. E., Hinton, G. E., & Williams, R. J. (1986). Learning representations by back-propagating errors. *Nature, 323*(6088), 533-536.
- Russell, S., & Norvig, P. (2016). *Artificial Intelligence: A Modern Approach*. Pearson.

- Silver, D., Huang, A., Maddison, C. J., Guez, A., Sifre, L., Van Den Driessche, G., ... & Hassabis, D. (2016). Mastering the game of Go with deep neural networks and tree search. *nature, 529*(7587), 484-489.
- Tesla. (2021). *Autopilot*. Retrieved from https://www.tesla.com/autopilot
- Turing, A. M. (1950). Computing machinery and intelligence. *Mind, 59*(236), 433-460.
- Von Ahn, L., Blum, M., & Langford, J. (2003). Telling humans and computers apart automatically. *Communications of the ACM, 47*(2), 56-60.
- Weizenbaum, J. (1966). ELIZA—a computer program for the study of natural language communication between man and machine. *Communications of the ACM, 9*(1), 36-45.
- West, D. M. (2018). *The Future of Work: Robots, AI, and Automation*. Brookings Institution Press.

Additional Reading

- Bessen, J. (2019). *AI and Jobs: The Role of Demand*. NBER Working Paper Series.
- Tegmark, M. (2017). *Life 3.0: Being Human in the Age of Artificial Intelligence*. Knopf.

Crafting Effective AI Strategies: From Objectives to Implementation

Abstract

This article explores the essential aspects of crafting and implementing practical AI strategies, emphasising the importance of clear objectives aligned with business goals. It delves into assessing organisational readiness, developing a comprehensive AI roadmap, building robust infrastructure, and establishing governance frameworks. The discussion highlights the significance of collaboration, continuous learning, and ethical practices in AI integration. By providing industry examples and practical insights, the article underscores the importance of iterative improvement and adaptation in AI strategy, ensuring sustained growth, innovation, and transformative business success.

Introduction

Artificial intelligence (AI) is a discipline that seeks to replicate or simulate human intelligence in machines, allowing them to perform tasks that typically require human cognitive abilities. Unlike natural intelligence exhibited by humans and animals, AI systems perform tasks using algorithms and data but do not learn and reason in the same way as humans. Currently, AI systems have very narrow capabilities, excelling at tasks but lacking the general adaptability of human intelligence.

Defining AI Strategy Objectives and Goals

Let us start by discussing the essential aspects of crafting practical AI strategies, objectives, and goals. Whether you're navigating the realm of business development or strategic planning, understanding these principles will be crucial in harnessing the power of artificial intelligence.

Firstly, let's clarify the importance of setting clear objectives. Think of AI strategy as a compass guiding your organisation towards specific outcomes. These objectives should align closely with your overall business goals, whether that's enhancing operational efficiency, improving customer experiences, or innovating your product offerings. When defining these objectives, consider the tangible benefits AI can bring. It's about leveraging AI to solve real business challenges and capitalise on opportunities that were previously out of reach. Moreover, goals in AI strategy should be SMART: Specific, Measurable, Achievable, Relevant, and Time-bound. This framework ensures that each objective is well-defined and actionable, facilitating better decision-making and resource allocation across your teams.

For instance, Amazon has leveraged AI to optimise its supply chain operations and enhance its recommendation systems, leading to increased efficiency and customer satisfaction (Stone, 2013). Similarly, Google has applied AI to refine its search algorithms and develop autonomous systems, showcasing the transformative potential of strategic AI implementation (Sullivan, 2016).

An important aspect often overlooked is the scalability of AI initiatives. As your organisation evolves, so too should your AI strategy. Scalability ensures that your objectives remain adaptable to changing market conditions and technological advancements, allowing for sustained growth and competitive advantage.

Additionally, the quality of data is foundational to the success of AI initiatives. High-quality data ensures that AI systems can produce reliable and actionable insights. Hence, investing in robust data management practices is crucial (Provost & Fawcett, 2013).

Furthermore, fostering a culture of data-driven decision-making is pivotal in achieving AI strategy goals. By integrating AI into your analytics processes, you empower your teams to derive actionable insights from vast amounts of data, enabling faster and more informed decision-making at all levels of the organisation.

Lastly, communication and collaboration are essential. Effective AI strategy requires alignment across departments and leadership. Everyone should understand how AI objectives support the broader organisational mission, fostering a cohesive approach towards implementation and success.

In conclusion, defining AI strategy objectives and goals is about technology, strategic foresight, and alignment with business imperatives. By setting clear objectives, leveraging scalable solutions, and fostering a data-driven culture, your organisation can harness the transformative power of AI to drive innovation and sustainable growth.

Assessing Organisational Readiness for AI Adoption

Let us explore how organisations can assess their readiness to adopt artificial intelligence, a crucial step in today's evolving business landscape. As seasoned leaders with decades of managerial experience, you understand the balance between innovation and practicality in achieving organisational goals.

Artificial intelligence offers significant benefits across industries, such as improving efficiency and uncovering new insights. However, successful integration depends on technology and on how prepared your organisation is to embrace and leverage AI effectively.

Firstly, assessing readiness involves evaluating your current systems and data practices. Consider your IT infrastructure: how reliable is it? Are your data management processes flexible enough for AI-driven initiatives? These questions form the foundation for AI implementation. For example, companies like Walmart have invested heavily in robust IT infrastructure and data management systems to support their AI initiatives (McMillon, 2021).

Secondly, think about your team. Your workforce is critical. Assessing readiness means understanding their skills and identifying any gaps AI adoption might reveal. This is about technical skills and understanding how AI can enhance its abilities to deliver more value for the organisation. A study by McKinsey found that organisations with strong AI capabilities were 50% more likely to achieve better business outcomes (Bughin et al., 2018). Consider providing training programs or hiring experts to bridge skill gaps.

Moreover, readiness requires a cultural shift. How open is your company culture to change and experimentation? AI adoption often demands a mindset of continuous learning and adaptation. Foster an environment where curiosity thrives and failures are seen as opportunities for improvement. Google's innovation culture is a prime example, where employees are encouraged to experiment and learn from failures (Schmidt & Rosenberg, 2014).

It's also crucial to align AI adoption with your strategic goals. How does AI support your long-term vision? Ensure AI initiatives are integrated into your broader business strategy to enhance competitiveness and sustainability. For instance, Siemens has integrated AI into its strategic planning to improve operational efficiency and innovation (Siemens AG, 2020).

Lastly, consider ethical and regulatory aspects. AI raises concerns like data privacy and bias. Being ready means having frameworks to handle these issues proactively. Implementing guidelines based on GDPR or other relevant regulations is essential to ensure compliance and build trust (Voigt & Von dem Bussche, 2017).

In conclusion, assessing readiness for AI adoption involves more than just technology—it's about overall preparedness. From infrastructure and workforce readiness to cultural alignment and strategic integration, these elements determine how effectively AI can drive innovation and growth in your organisation. By addressing these areas, you can pave the way for successful AI implementation that aligns with your organisational goals and values.

Aligning AI Strategy with Business Goals and Vision

A critical aspect of modern business is aligning your strategic vision with the power of artificial intelligence (AI). Over the past decade, technology has dramatically reshaped industries, and AI is leading this change. For seasoned professionals, understanding how AI can drive business goals is essential for staying competitive and innovative.

Let's start by explaining what it means to align AI strategy with business goals and vision. This involves using AI as a strategic asset that enhances your organisation's strengths. As experienced leaders, you understand that every decision should align with the company's goals and how to achieve them.

In this context, AI acts as a powerful enabler for reaching those goals. Whether it's improving efficiency, enhancing customer experiences, or identifying new growth opportunities, AI can significantly impact your business. This is more than just adopting a new technology—it's about integrating AI into your strategy to help your business adapt and thrive in a changing environment.

Consider the example of Netflix, which uses AI algorithms to personalise content recommendations for its users. This alignment of AI with their business goal of enhancing customer experience has resulted in increased user engagement and retention (Amatriain, 2013).

Now, you might wonder how to align AI strategy without a technical background. Your expertise is in leadership, strategy, and market dynamics—not in coding or algorithms.

The good news is that successful AI integration begins with asking the right questions and working effectively with your technical teams. It's about defining challenges in a way that allows AI to offer solutions without getting lost in technical details.

Instead of focusing on the technical aspects of AI, think about how AI can solve specific business challenges. For instance, a retail company like Walmart leverages AI for inventory management to ensure products are available when customers need them, directly supporting their goal of optimising supply chain efficiency (Hays, Keskinocak, & de Lopez, 2005).

Moreover, creating a culture that embraces AI requires clear communication and change management. As leaders, your role is to support AI adoption and to ensure your teams understand its potential and have the skills to use it effectively. This might involve investing in training programs or working with external experts who can provide tailored advice.

An example of successful AI adoption is how JP Morgan Chase implemented AI to streamline its contract review process through a system called COIN, which has saved thousands of hours of legal work (JPMorgan Chase & Co., 2017). This aligns with their goal of operational efficiency and frees up human resources for more complex tasks.

In conclusion, aligning AI strategy with business goals is a journey that demands strategic thinking, collaboration, and continuous learning. As experienced leaders, you have the insight and leadership skills to guide your organisation towards a future where AI complements human ingenuity.

By integrating AI into your strategic framework, you position your company for success today and lay the foundation for sustained growth and innovation in the future.

Developing a Roadmap for AI Implementation

Now, let us explore how to develop a comprehensive roadmap for AI implementation in your organisation, ensuring a smooth and effective transition to this transformative technology. With decades of experience under your belt, it's crucial to grasp the strategic aspects of AI adoption without needing to delve into the technical details. Let me guide you through a structured approach, using the latest industry examples to illustrate key points.

First, define the specific business objectives you aim to achieve with AI. Whether it's enhancing customer service, optimising supply chain operations, or driving product innovation, clear goals will direct your AI strategy. For example, Amazon uses AI to streamline its logistics and delivery systems, resulting in faster shipping times and reduced operational costs (Agarwal, 2020). By identifying targeted outcomes, you can align

AI initiatives with your broader business strategy.

Next, evaluate the current state of your data infrastructure. AI relies heavily on data, so having a solid data management system is essential. This means assessing data quality, availability, and governance. Companies like Netflix use advanced data analytics to predict viewer preferences, tailor content recommendations, and improve user experience. Investing in data readiness will create a strong foundation for AI projects (Gomez-Uribe & Hunt, 2016).

Building a cross-functional team is another critical step. AI implementation requires collaboration across various departments, including IT, operations, and human resources. A team with diverse expertise ensures that all aspects of the project are covered. For example, Pfizer's AI-driven drug discovery initiatives benefit from the combined efforts of biologists, data scientists, and IT specialists, speeding up the development of new medicines (Bianconi, 2020).

Pilot projects are an excellent way to test AI applications on a smaller scale before full-scale deployment. Start with projects that have a high potential for impact but are manageable in scope. This way, you can learn from initial experiences, refine your approach, and demonstrate tangible benefits to stakeholders. Google's use of AI in optimising data centre energy efficiency started as a pilot and expanded company-wide after proving its value, resulting in significant cost savings and environmental benefits (Gao, 2014).

As you move from pilot to full-scale implementation, focus on scalability and integration. Ensure that AI solutions can handle increased loads and work seamlessly with existing systems. A phased approach, where AI capabilities are gradually introduced, can help manage risks and facilitate smoother adoption. Consider JPMorgan Chase, which integrated AI to enhance fraud detection. By gradually scaling their AI systems, they effectively mitigated risks while improving security (Chui, 2018).

Monitoring and evaluation are crucial components of the AI roadmap. Continuous performance assessment helps identify areas for improvement and ensures that AI systems are delivering the expected outcomes. Setting up key performance indicators (KPIs) and regular review processes will keep the implementation on track. IBM Watson's application in healthcare, where it assists in diagnosing diseases and recommending treatments, is constantly refined based on feedback and performance metrics, ensuring its accuracy and reliability (Ferrucci, 2012).

Finally, fostering a culture of innovation and continuous learning is essential for sustained success in AI adoption. Encourage your team to stay updated with the latest AI trends and advancements. Investing in training and development programs will empower your workforce to leverage AI effectively. For instance, Microsoft's AI Business School provides resources and training to help leaders understand and implement AI strategies successfully (Microsoft, 2019).

In conclusion, developing a roadmap for AI implementation involves setting clear objectives, preparing your data infrastructure, building a cross-functional team, starting with pilot projects, focusing on scalability, monitoring performance, and fostering a culture of continuous learning. By following these steps and drawing inspiration from industry leaders, you can successfully navigate the complexities of AI adoption and drive significant business value.

Building AI Infrastructure and Capabilities

Now, we delve into the essential components and strategies for building AI infrastructure and capabilities within your organisation. With the rapid advancements in artificial intelligence, establishing a robust AI foundation is a competitive advantage and a necessity. We'll explore how to lay down this

foundation effectively, focusing on practical insights and real-world examples from leading companies.

To begin with, it's crucial to understand that AI infrastructure is the backbone that supports the development, deployment, and scaling of AI applications. This infrastructure encompasses hardware, software, data storage, and networking capabilities. One notable example is Google's Tensor Processing Unit (TPU), a custom-built application-specific integrated circuit (ASIC) designed to accelerate machine learning workloads. By investing in specialised hardware like TPUs, Google has significantly enhanced its AI processing power, enabling faster and more efficient machine learning operations (Jouppi et al., 2017). Another example is NVIDIA's GPUs, which are widely used across the industry for their parallel processing capabilities that are ideal for deep learning tasks (Woolley, 2019).

Next, let's talk about data—the lifeblood of AI. High-quality, diverse data sets are essential for training robust AI models. Take Amazon, for instance. Amazon leverages vast amounts of customer data to power its recommendation engines, which are among the most sophisticated in the world. By continuously refining these models with new data, Amazon ensures that its recommendations remain relevant and personalised, driving customer satisfaction and sales (Smith & Linden, 2017).

However, it's more than just having data; it's about having the proper data infrastructure to manage and process this data efficiently. This is where data lakes and data warehouses come into play. Companies like Netflix have mastered the art of data management by building a scalable, cloud-based data infrastructure. Netflix's data infrastructure supports real-time analytics, enabling the company to deliver personalised content recommendations to its millions of users worldwide (Narkhede et al., 2017).

Once the infrastructure is in place, developing AI capabilities requires a strategic approach to talent acquisition and development. Companies like Microsoft have invested heavily in upskilling their workforce, offering continuous learning opportunities in AI and machine learning. By fostering a culture of innovation and constant learning, Microsoft ensures that its teams are equipped with the latest AI skills and knowledge, which is crucial for staying ahead in the AI race (Microsoft, 2020). Additionally, organisations are increasingly leveraging AI platforms and tools such as TensorFlow, PyTorch, and Hugging Face to streamline their AI development processes.

Moreover, collaboration and partnerships play a pivotal role in building AI capabilities. IBM, for instance, has formed strategic alliances with academic institutions and research organisations to drive AI innovation. By collaborating with external experts, IBM can tap into cutting-edge research and technologies, accelerating its AI development efforts (IBM Research, 2021). Similarly, Google has established AI research partnerships with universities worldwide to foster innovation and explore new AI frontiers (Dean, 2019).

It's also important to focus on ethical AI practices. AI systems must be designed and deployed responsibly to ensure fairness, transparency, and accountability. One example of a company leading the way in ethical AI is Microsoft, which has established an AI Ethics Committee to oversee its AI initiatives. This committee ensures that Microsoft's AI technologies are developed and used in ways that align with ethical guidelines and societal values (Smith, 2018). Additionally, Google has implemented the AI Principles, a set of policies designed to ensure responsible AI development and use (Pichai, 2018).

Finally, let's consider the importance of a robust AI strategy. A well-defined AI strategy aligns AI initiatives with business goals, ensuring that AI investments deliver tangible value. For instance, BMW has integrated AI into its manufacturing processes to optimise production efficiency and quality control. By strategically deploying AI, BMW has enhanced its operational performance and maintained its competitive edge in the automotive industry (Krishnakumar, 2020). Another example is Unilever, which uses AI to optimise its supply chain and predict consumer trends, significantly improving its operational efficiency and responsiveness to market changes (Unilever, 2018).

In summary, building AI infrastructure and capabilities involves a multifaceted approach that includes investing in the proper hardware and software, managing and leveraging data effectively, fostering talent and collaboration, adhering to ethical practices, and aligning AI initiatives with business goals. By learning from the successes of industry leaders like Google, Amazon, Netflix, Microsoft, IBM, BMW, and Unilever, organisations can develop a solid AI foundation that drives innovation and growth.

Establishing AI Governance and Compliance Frameworks

Let us now discuss how to set up AI governance and compliance frameworks in your organisation. As AI becomes a more significant part of business operations, it's crucial to have rules and procedures to manage its use responsibly. This discussion will help you understand how to create and implement these frameworks effectively.

AI governance involves setting policies and standards to ensure AI is used ethically and responsibly. This includes areas like data privacy, fairness in decision-making, and accountability. Compliance frameworks make sure that AI systems follow legal and regulatory requirements, reducing risks and protecting everyone's interests. It is also essential to consider the broader societal impact of AI, including biases in AI systems and ensuring inclusivity.

For example, the European Union is working on AI regulations called the AI Act. This law aims to ensure that AI is safe, transparent, and accountable. It classifies AI applications based on risk levels and sets specific requirements for each category (European Commission, 2021). Companies like Siemens are already updating their AI strategies to comply with these upcoming regulations. In the United States, the Algorithmic Accountability Act is another significant legislative effort aimed at regulating AI and automated decision systems, requiring companies to evaluate the impact of their AI technologies (House of Representatives, 2019).

To establish a practical AI governance framework, start by defining clear ethical guidelines. IBM's AI Ethics Board, for instance, has principles like fairness, transparency, and privacy. These principles should be the foundation of your governance framework (IBM, 2019).

It's essential to create a cross-functional governance team. This team should include members from legal, compliance, IT, and business units. They will oversee AI projects and ensure they meet ethical standards and regulatory requirements. Regular training sessions can keep the team updated on the latest AI advancements and best practices.

Transparency in AI decision-making is essential. Stakeholders need to understand how AI systems make decisions, especially in sensitive areas like healthcare or finance. For example, Deloitte has developed a documentation framework that explains how AI models work and how decisions are made. Adopting similar practices can build trust and ensure accountability (Deloitte, 2018).

Implementing robust monitoring and auditing systems is another critical step. Regular audits can identify any deviations from established guidelines. Google, for instance, has an internal audit process to review AI projects and ensure they comply with ethical and regulatory standards (Google AI, 2019).

Additionally, Microsoft has implemented a Responsible AI dashboard that helps monitor the performance and fairness of AI models, providing transparency and accountability (Microsoft, 2020).

Keeping up with the rapidly changing regulatory landscape is also essential. In the United States, the National Institute of Standards and Technology (NIST) is developing a framework to manage AI risks. Staying informed about such developments can help your organisation anticipate changes and adjust your AI strategies accordingly (NIST, 2020). Globally, the Organisation for Economic Co-operation and Development (OECD) has established AI principles that provide a framework for AI governance, focusing on areas such as human-centred values, transparency, and accountability (OECD, 2019).

In summary, setting up AI governance and compliance frameworks requires a strategic approach based on ethical principles, teamwork, transparency, regular audits, and staying informed about regulations. As AI continues to evolve and impact industries, having a solid governance framework will be crucial for using AI responsibly and ethically. This proactive approach will reduce risks and promote innovation and trust in AI systems.

Identifying Key Stakeholders and Roles in AI Strategy Execution

We now delve into the critical task of identifying key stakeholders and their roles in the successful execution of AI strategies. This is about ensuring your organisation harnesses the full potential of artificial intelligence in a strategic and impactful way.

Imagine orchestrating a symphony where each player, with their unique skills and instruments, contributes to a harmonious outcome. Similarly, in AI strategy, every stakeholder plays a crucial role from conception to implementation.

Let's start with a compelling example from the financial sector. JP Morgan Chase, a global leader in banking, recognised early on that AI could revolutionise their operations. They identified stakeholders ranging from data scientists to compliance officers, ensuring every aspect of AI integration was covered. This strategic approach enhanced customer service through predictive analytics and optimised risk management, thanks to proactive AI-driven insights (JP Morgan Chase & Co., 2018).

Identifying stakeholders begins with understanding who stands to benefit or be impacted by AI initiatives. This includes business unit heads, marketing leads, legal advisors, and, of course, technology specialists. Each brings a unique perspective that shapes how AI is adopted and utilised within your organisation.

Take the case of Salesforce, a pioneer in customer relationship management. Their AI strategy involved collaboration across departments, from sales and customer support to IT and product development. By involving stakeholders early on, they aligned AI capabilities with business objectives, creating tailored solutions that boosted customer satisfaction and operational efficiency (Salesforce, 2020).

Roles in AI strategy execution vary but are equally vital. Business leaders define the overarching goals and outcomes, ensuring AI aligns with corporate strategy. Data scientists and analysts provide the technical expertise to interpret complex data and develop AI models. Meanwhile, project managers keep timelines on track, ensuring smooth integration and deployment. Additionally, AI ethicists and compliance officers ensure that AI implementations adhere to ethical standards and regulatory requirements.

Consider Amazon's AI initiatives, where Jeff Bezos famously mandated that every team integrate AI into their operations. This directive empowered teams across logistics, retail, and cloud services to innovate with AI, driving efficiency and customer experience

improvements across the board (Bezos, 2017).

Moreover, stakeholders aren't confined to internal teams alone. Collaborating with external partners such as AI vendors, consultants, and industry experts can bring fresh perspectives and specialised knowledge to your AI strategy. This external collaboration was pivotal for Toyota when they partnered with NVIDIA to enhance their autonomous driving systems, leveraging NVIDIA's AI expertise to accelerate innovation and safety in their vehicles (NVIDIA, 2019).

Lastly, communication among stakeholders is paramount. Clear, ongoing dialogue ensures that AI initiatives remain aligned with evolving business needs and regulatory requirements. This proactive approach was evident in Google's AI ethics board, where stakeholders debated the implications of AI applications, ensuring alignment with societal values and legal frameworks (Google AI, 2020). Practical communication tools and platforms, such as Slack or Microsoft Teams, can facilitate seamless interaction among stakeholders, ensuring everyone is on the same page.

In conclusion, identifying key stakeholders and defining their roles is the cornerstone of a successful AI strategy. By fostering collaboration, leveraging diverse expertise, and maintaining clear communication, organisations can navigate the complexities of AI adoption with confidence and achieve transformative outcomes.

Measuring and Evaluating the Success of AI Strategy Implementation

A crucial aspect of modern business strategy is measuring and evaluating the success of AI implementation. Over the past decade, many of you have witnessed the rapid evolution of technology within our industries, fundamentally reshaping how we operate. Let us explore how to effectively gauge the impact of these advancements without diving into technical jargon.

Let's start by understanding the essence of AI strategy implementation. It's more than just about adopting new technologies; it's about transforming our workflows, enhancing decision-making processes, and ultimately driving tangible business outcomes. Take the example of Netflix, which uses AI to personalise recommendations. This strategic use of AI has significantly boosted customer satisfaction and retention rates, directly translating into revenue growth (Gomez-Uribe & Hunt, 2015). Another example is Alibaba, which employs AI to enhance its supply chain efficiency and customer service, resulting in substantial operational improvements and customer satisfaction (Alibaba Group, 2018).

Now, how do we measure success in this context? Traditionally, success metrics might have been straightforward, like ROI or cost savings. However, AI has become more nuanced. It involves looking at both quantitative and qualitative indicators. For instance, quantitative metrics could include efficiency gains in operational processes or revenue generated through AI-driven initiatives.

Qualitative indicators, on the other hand, are equally crucial. They involve assessing the impact on customer experience, employee satisfaction, and even brand perception. Companies like Starbucks have leveraged AI to optimise store operations and tailor customer interactions, enhancing brand loyalty through personalised services (Starbucks, 2019).

To ensure meaningful evaluation, it's vital to establish clear benchmarks from the outset. This means defining what success looks like before implementation begins. It could reduce response times in customer service by a certain percentage or improve forecast accuracy in supply chain management. Moreover, ongoing monitoring and adaptation are essential. AI is not a static tool; it evolves alongside our business needs and external dynamics. For example, Amazon continuously adjusts its AI algorithms to meet changing consumer behaviours, ensuring relevance and effectiveness in dynamic markets (Levy, 2017).

Another critical aspect is transparency and accountability. As leaders, fostering a culture where AI outcomes are transparently communicated and understood across teams fosters trust and alignment. This openness also enables continuous improvement and refinement of AI strategies over time.

Ultimately, the success of AI strategy lies in its integration into our organisational DNA. It's a mindset shift towards data-driven decision-making and innovation. Companies like Google have embedded AI into their strategic vision, leading to sustainable competitive advantages and continuous innovation (Dean, 2019).

In conclusion, measuring and evaluating AI strategy implementation requires a blend of foresight, adaptability, and a keen understanding of both quantitative metrics and qualitative impacts. By staying attuned to these principles and learning from real-world examples, we can navigate this transformative journey with confidence and clarity.

Iterative Improvement and Adaptation of AI Strategy

Lastly, we will dive into a crucial aspect of refining your approach to artificial intelligence: Iterative Improvement and Adaptation. Imagine your business strategy as a dynamic puzzle, where each piece represents an opportunity to enhance and adjust your AI initiatives over time.

Think back to companies like Amazon and Netflix. Both have transformed their industries by continually refining their AI strategies. For instance, Amazon's recommendation algorithms have evolved significantly from basic product suggestions to highly personalised experiences that boost sales and customer satisfaction. Similarly, Netflix analyses viewer habits in real time to recommend shows, keeping subscribers engaged and reducing churn. Another example is Spotify, which iterates on its recommendation algorithms to provide personalised music suggestions, enhancing user engagement and satisfaction (Covington, Adams, & Sargin, 2016).

These examples illustrate the power of iterative improvement. It's not just about implementing AI once and considering it done. Instead, it's a journey of ongoing adjustments based on real-world feedback and technological advancements.

Now, let's break down how iterative improvement works in practical terms. Imagine launching an AI-driven customer service chatbot. Initially, it may handle basic inquiries, but through continuous monitoring and feedback analysis, you can refine its responses to be more accurate and helpful. This iterative process ensures that your AI exceeds customer expectations over time.

Consider the healthcare sector, where AI is revolutionising patient care. Hospitals are using AI to analyse medical images, leading to faster and more accurate diagnoses. But it doesn't stop there. Continuous refinement of these algorithms means better outcomes for patients and more efficient use of medical staff's time (Esteva et al., 2017).

As someone with a wealth of experience, you understand the value of strategic adaptation. Just as you've adapted to changing market dynamics and business environments over the years, so too must your approach to AI evolve. It's about staying ahead of the curve and leveraging AI as a competitive advantage.

Let's look at the automotive industry, where AI-powered autonomous vehicles are becoming a reality. Companies like Waymo are not just developing autonomous vehicles; they're iterating on their AI systems to improve safety and efficiency continuously. Updates are rolled out over the air, enhancing the driving experience without requiring physical modifications (Waymo, 2018).

In your leadership role, you can foster a culture of continuous improvement around AI. Encourage your teams to experiment, gather data, and use insights to refine their strategies. It's this iterative approach that allows companies to stay innovative and responsive in a rapidly changing technological landscape.

Remember, the key to a successful AI strategy lies not in a single deployment but in the ongoing process of adaptation and enhancement. By embracing iterative improvement, you're not just keeping pace with the competition—you're setting the pace.

So, as you reflect on your journey and the lessons learned over the years, consider how you can apply the principles of iterative improvement to your organisation's AI strategy. It's a journey that promises both challenges and rewards but one that ultimately leads to greater efficiency, innovation, and success.

Conclusion

Effectively harnessing AI within an organisation requires strategic foresight, continuous adaptation, and alignment with business objectives. Clear AI strategy objectives drive operational efficiency, customer experience enhancements, and innovation. Assessing readiness for AI adoption involves evaluating technological infrastructure, data quality, workforce capabilities, and cultural openness. Successful AI integration demands collaboration across departments, clear communication, and a strategic approach to problem-solving.

A comprehensive roadmap for AI implementation includes setting objectives, evaluating data infrastructure, building cross-functional teams, starting with pilot projects, focusing on scalability, and fostering continuous learning. Robust AI infrastructure and capabilities require investment in hardware, software, effective data management, talent development, and adherence to ethical practices.

Establishing AI governance and compliance frameworks ensures responsible and ethical AI use that aligns with legal requirements. Identifying key stakeholders and their roles is crucial for executing AI strategies, fostering collaboration, and leveraging diverse expertise. Measuring and evaluating AI strategy success involves understanding quantitative and qualitative impacts and continuous adaptation.

Finally, iterative improvement and adaptation of AI strategy emphasise ongoing adjustments based on feedback and technological advancements. A strategic and adaptive approach, grounded in clear objectives, robust infrastructure, and continuous learning, ensures AI drives sustained growth and innovation, becoming a catalyst for transformative business success.

References

- Agarwal, A. (2020). *The Impact of Artificial Intelligence on Supply Chain*

Management: A Case Study of Amazon. Supply Chain Management Review.
- Alibaba Group. (2018). *Alibaba's New Retail Strategy: Integrating Online and Offline Shopping*. Retrieved from https://www.alibabagroup.com
- Amatriain, X. (2013). *Big & Personal: Data and Models Behind Netflix Recommendations*. Proceedings of the 2nd International Workshop on Big Data, Streams and Heterogeneous Source Mining: Algorithms, Systems, Programming Models and Applications.
- Bezos, J. (2017). *2016 Letter to Shareholders*. Amazon.
- Bianconi, G. (2020). *Pfizer's AI-driven Drug Discovery Initiatives*. BioTechniques.
- Bughin, J., Hazan, E., Ramaswamy, S., Chui, M., Allas, T., Dahlström, P., ... Trench, M. (2018). *Artificial Intelligence: The Next Digital Frontier?* McKinsey Global Institute.
- Chui, M. (2018). *AI Fraud Detection at JPMorgan Chase*. McKinsey Quarterly.

- Covington, P., Adams, J., & Sargin, E. (2016). *Deep Neural Networks for YouTube Recommendations*. Proceedings of the 10th ACM Conference on Recommender Systems.
- Dean, J. (2019). *Building and Using Machine Learning at Scale*. Google AI Blog.
- Deloitte. (2018). *Artificial Intelligence Documentation Framework*. Deloitte Insights.
- Esteva, A., Kuprel, B., Novoa, R. A., Ko, J., Swetter, S. M., Blau, H. M., & Thrun, S. (2017). *Dermatologist-level Classification of Skin Cancer with Deep Neural Networks*. Nature.
- European Commission. (2021). *Proposal for a Regulation Laying Down Harmonised Rules on Artificial Intelligence (Artificial Intelligence Act)*. European Union.
- Ferrucci, D. (2012). *Introduction to "This is Watson"*. IBM Journal of Research and Development.

- Gao, J. (2014). *Google's Data Center Efficiency and Machine Learning*. Google Cloud Blog.
- Gomez-Uribe, C. A., & Hunt, N. (2015). *The Netflix Recommender System: Algorithms, Business Value, and Innovation*. ACM Transactions on Management Information Systems.
- Google AI. (2019). *Responsible AI Practices*. Google.
- Google AI. (2020). *AI Ethics Board Annual Report*. Google.
- Hays, H. M., Keskinocak, P., & de Lopez, A. R. (2005). *Strategic Inventory Placement in Supply Chains: Walmart Case Study*. Supply Chain Management: An International Journal.
- House of Representatives. (2019). *Algorithmic Accountability Act of 2019*. Congress.gov.
- IBM Research. (2021). *Collaborative AI Research at IBM*. IBM Research Blog.
- IBM. (2019). *IBM AI Ethics Board Guidelines*. IBM.

- Jouppi, N. P., Young, C., Patil, N., Patterson, D., Agrawal, G., Bajwa, R., ... & Laudon, J. (2017). *In-Datacenter Performance Analysis of a Tensor Processing Unit*. Proceedings of the 44th Annual International Symposium on Computer Architecture.
- JP Morgan Chase & Co. (2017). *Introducing COIN: Contract Intelligence*. JP Morgan Chase & Co.
- JP Morgan Chase & Co. (2018). *AI-driven Customer Service Enhancements*. JP Morgan Chase & Co.
- Krishnakumar, P. (2020). *AI in BMW Manufacturing: Optimizing Efficiency and Quality*. Automotive News.
- Levy, S. (2017). *Amazon's AI Future: From Alexa to Beyond*. Wired.
- McMillon, D. (2021). *Walmart's Technology Transformation*. Harvard Business Review.
- Microsoft. (2019). *AI Business School: Executive Briefing*. Microsoft.

- Microsoft. (2020). *Responsible AI Practices and Ethics Dashboard*. Microsoft.
- Narkhede, N., Raine, J., & Shapira, T. (2017). *Data Infrastructure at Netflix: Real-Time Analytics and Beyond*. Proceedings of the 43rd International Conference on Very Large Data Bases.
- NIST. (2020). *AI Risk Management Framework*. National Institute of Standards and Technology.
- NVIDIA. (2019). *NVIDIA AI in Autonomous Vehicles*. NVIDIA Blog.
- OECD. (2019). *Recommendation of the Council on Artificial Intelligence*. OECD Legal Instruments.
- Pichai, S. (2018). *AI at Google: Our Principles*. Google Blog.
- Provost, F., & Fawcett, T. (2013). *Data Science for Business: What You Need to Know About Data Mining and Data-Analytic Thinking*. O'Reilly Media.
- Salesforce. (2020). *AI-Driven Customer Relationship Management at Salesforce*. Salesforce Research.

- Schmidt, E., & Rosenberg, J. (2014). *How Google Works*. Grand Central Publishing.
- Siemens AG. (2020). *Strategic AI Integration at Siemens*. Siemens AG.
- Smith, B. (2018). *The Future Computed: Artificial Intelligence and its Role in Society*. Microsoft.
- Smith, B., & Linden, G. (2017). *Two Decades of Recommender Systems at Amazon.com*. IEEE Internet Computing.
- Starbucks. (2019). *How Starbucks Uses AI to Enhance Customer Experience*. Starbucks Stories & News.
- Sullivan, D. (2016). *How Google's Search Engine Really Works*. Search Engine Land.
- Unilever. (2018). *AI-Driven Supply Chain Optimisation at Unilever*. Unilever News.

Additional Reading

- Bostrom, N. (2014). *Superintelligence: Paths, Dangers, Strategies*. Oxford University Press.
- Brynjolfsson, E., & McAfee, A. (2014). *The Second Machine Age: Work, Progress, and Prosperity in a Time of Brilliant Technologies*. W. W. Norton & Company.
- Goodfellow, I., Bengio, Y., & Courville, A. (2016). *Deep Learning*. MIT Press.
- Manyika, J., Chui, M., Miremadi, M., Bughin, J., George, K., Willmott, P., & Dewhurst, M. (2017). *A Future That Works: Automation, Employment, and Productivity*. McKinsey Global Institute.
- Tegmark, M. (2017). *Life 3.0: Being Human in the Age of Artificial Intelligence*. Knopf.
- West, D. M. (2018). *The Future of Work: Robots, AI, and Automation*. Brookings Institution Press.

Transforming Business Operations with AI Integration

Abstract

Artificial Intelligence (AI) is revolutionising business operations by significantly enhancing decision-making, operational efficiency, and strategic planning. This article delves into the necessity of integrating AI into modern business practices, highlighting its transformative capabilities. It examines the role of data, automation, personalised customer experiences, risk management, and the strategic approach required for successful AI integration. The discussion includes real-world case studies, best practices for managing change, ensuring data security, and exploring future trends in AI technologies and practices. The conclusion emphasises AI's role in augmenting human capabilities, driving innovation, and maintaining a competitive edge in the business landscape.

Introduction

Artificial Intelligence (AI) has emerged as a crucial element in modern business operations, transforming how organisations make decisions, enhance operational efficiency, and execute strategic planning. For professionals with extensive experience in management, understanding and leveraging AI can drive substantial growth and maintain competitiveness in an evolving business landscape. This article explores the fundamental aspects of AI integration, its benefits, challenges, and the strategic approach necessary for successful implementation.

The Importance of Data

Every organisation generates vast amounts of data daily, holding invaluable insights that can drive better business decisions. Traditional data analysis methods often fall short due to the volume and complexity of the data. AI algorithms can process and analyse massive datasets at unprecedented speeds, uncovering patterns and trends that would be difficult for humans to detect manually. By integrating AI, businesses can gain actionable insights in real time, leading to more informed and timely decisions (Russell & Norvig, 2016). Ensuring data quality and preprocessing is crucial for accurate and reliable AI-driven insights.

Enhancing Operational Efficiency

AI enhances operational efficiency by automating routine and repetitive tasks. AI-powered chatbots can handle customer inquiries around the clock, freeing up human resources for more complex and value-added tasks. Similarly, AI can optimise supply chain management by predicting demand, identifying potential disruptions, and suggesting optimal routes and inventory levels. This level of automation reduces operational costs and improves service quality and customer satisfaction (Manyika et al., 2017).

Personalising Customer Experiences

In today's competitive market, understanding and anticipating customer needs is crucial. AI can analyse customer behaviour and preferences to provide personalised recommendations and experiences. This boosts customer loyalty and drives sales and revenue growth. For instance, e-commerce platforms use AI to recommend products based on past purchases and browsing history, enhancing the shopping experience and increasing conversion rates (Gandomi & Haider, 2015).

Risk Management and Fraud Detection

AI plays a pivotal role in risk management and fraud detection. By continuously monitoring transactions and activities, AI systems can identify unusual patterns and flag potential fraud or security breaches. This proactive approach to risk management helps protect the organisation's assets and reputation, ensuring long-term sustainability. AI applications are also used in cybersecurity, such as anomaly detection in network traffic and AI-driven incident response systems (Mayer-Schönberger & Cukier, 2013).

Challenges in AI Integration

Integrating AI into business operations is not without its challenges. A strategic approach is required, starting with a clear understanding of the specific problems AI can solve within the organisation. Fostering a culture of innovation and continuous learning is essential, encouraging teams to embrace new technologies and adapt to changes. Investing in the right AI tools and platforms, as well as upskilling the workforce, are critical steps in this journey. Ethical AI practices and governance frameworks are essential to ensure responsible and fair use of AI technologies (Bostrom, 2014).

Case Studies

Real-world case studies illustrate the diverse applications and significant benefits of AI integration across various industries.

Walmart is one of the largest retail chains globally, leveraging big data to optimise operations and enhance customer experiences. Walmart processes over 2.5 petabytes of data every hour, generated from transactions, social media, and sensors. This data is analysed in real-time to manage inventory, predict customer preferences, and personalise marketing efforts. Using big data analytics, Walmart can quickly respond to market changes, ensuring popular products are in stock and reducing waste from overstocking (Manyika et al., 2017).

Netflix uses big data analytics to recommend content to its users. Collecting data on viewing habits, search queries, and even the time of day users watch content, Netflix processes this information to create personalised recommendations, enhancing user experience and engagement. By analysing big data, Netflix can predict what shows or movies a user is likely to enjoy, leading to higher satisfaction and retention rates. The use of big data has been a critical factor in Netflix's success, allowing it to deliver a tailored viewing experience to millions of subscribers worldwide (Gandomi & Haider, 2015).

Best Practices for AI Integration

Integrating AI into business operations requires a clear vision and purpose. It is crucial to communicate how AI will benefit the organisation, enhance processes, and contribute to overall goals. This transparency builds trust and aligns everyone with the same objectives. Establishing a well-defined purpose clarifies the rationale behind the change and helps anticipate and address concerns that may arise during the transition.

Creating a culture that embraces change and innovation is essential. Encourage a mindset that views AI as a tool for augmenting human capabilities rather than a threat to jobs. Regular training sessions, workshops, and open forums where employees can express their concerns, ask questions, and gain a deeper understanding of AI technologies are vital. Providing educational resources and learning opportunities ensures that everyone is equipped with the knowledge and skills needed to adapt to new AI-driven processes.

Involving key stakeholders in the planning and implementation phases is critical. Collaborate with team members from various departments to gather insights and feedback. This inclusive approach ensures that AI integration is comprehensive and considers the diverse needs of the organisation. Engaging stakeholders early in the process fosters a sense of ownership and commitment, which is essential for successful change management.

Effective communication is paramount. Develop a robust communication plan that outlines the timeline, milestones, and expected outcomes of AI integration. Regular updates and transparent communication help manage expectations and reduce uncertainties. Utilise multiple communication channels such as emails, intranet portals, and town hall meetings to keep everyone informed and engaged.

Implementing AI solutions incrementally can significantly mitigate risks associated with AI integration. Start with pilot projects to test AI applications in controlled environments. This allows for identifying potential issues and making necessary adjustments before a full-scale rollout. Pilot projects also provide tangible examples of AI benefits, which can help in gaining broader acceptance and support within the organisation. Notable examples include how UPS used pilot AI projects to optimise delivery routes, saving fuel costs and improving delivery times significantly.

Addressing ethical and regulatory aspects of AI integration is also essential. Ensure that AI solutions adhere to relevant laws and regulations and establish ethical guidelines to govern their use. This includes considerations around data privacy, algorithmic transparency, and fairness. Proactively addressing these issues builds a foundation of trust and accountability.

Continuously monitoring and evaluating the impact of AI on the organisation is crucial. Establish metrics and KPIs to measure the performance and outcomes of AI initiatives.

Regular assessments help identify areas for improvement and ensure that AI integration aligns with organisational goals. Be prepared to make iterative changes based on feedback and performance data to optimise the benefits of AI.

Ensuring Data Security and Privacy

Data security and privacy are paramount in AI integration. Understanding the types of data being handled is crucial. AI systems often process vast amounts of data, including personal, financial, and proprietary information. Identifying and classifying data based on its sensitivity can help implement appropriate security measures. This classification enables the development of tailored strategies to protect different data types.

One foundational step in ensuring data security is encryption. Encrypting data at rest and in transit ensures that even if

unauthorised access occurs, the data remains unreadable and secure. Utilising robust encryption algorithms and regularly updating encryption keys are essential practices. Additionally, employing secure communication protocols such as HTTPS and TLS can protect data during transmission (Russom, 2011).

Access control is another vital aspect. Implementing strict access controls ensures that only authorised personnel can access sensitive data. This can be achieved through multi-factor authentication, role-based access control, and regular audits of access logs. Limiting data access based on the principle of least privilege minimises the risk of data breaches (Russell & Norvig, 2016).

Data anonymisation and pseudonymisation are effective techniques for protecting privacy. By anonymising data, personally identifiable information is removed, reducing the risk of identification in case of a data breach. Pseudonymisation replaces sensitive data with pseudonyms, allowing for data analysis without exposing the actual data. These techniques are instrumental in complying with privacy regulations such as GDPR and CPRA. For instance, a healthcare provider implementing AI for patient data analysis can use anonymisation techniques to comply with HIPAA regulations, ensuring patient identities are protected while leveraging valuable data insights (Gandomi & Haider, 2015).

AI integration also requires continuous monitoring and auditing. Regularly monitoring AI systems for unusual activity can help detect potential security threats early. Implementing automated auditing tools can provide real-time insights into data access patterns and alert administrators to anomalies. Conducting periodic security assessments and vulnerability tests ensures that AI systems remain secure and compliant with evolving security standards (Mayer-Schönberger & Cukier, 2013).

Ensuring data integrity is critical. Data integrity refers to maintaining the accuracy and consistency of data throughout its lifecycle. Implementing checksums, digital signatures, and blockchain technology can help verify data integrity. Ensuring that data has not been tampered with is essential for making reliable decisions based on AI-generated insights (Russell & Norvig, 2016).

Training and awareness are indispensable in fostering a culture of data security. Educating employees about the importance of data security and privacy and best practices for handling sensitive data is crucial. Regular training sessions and workshops can keep everyone informed about the latest security threats and mitigation strategies. A well-informed workforce is a significant line of defence against potential security breaches (Manyika et al., 2017).

Data security is constantly evolving, with new threats and regulatory requirements emerging regularly. Keeping abreast of these changes ensures that AI systems and data protection measures remain robust and compliant. Participating in industry forums, subscribing to security bulletins, and collaborating with security experts can provide valuable insights and help maintain a solid security posture (Russell & Norvig, 2016).

Future Trends in AI Integration

The future of AI integration is shaped by several key trends that promise to drive significant advancements and innovations across industries. Understanding and staying ahead of these trends can position organisations at the forefront of technological transformation.

The increasing adoption of AI-driven automation is one such trend. Automation has already revolutionised numerous sectors, but the next wave will see more sophisticated AI algorithms automating complex decision-making processes. This will enhance efficiency and enable the handling of tasks that were previously thought to be the exclusive domain of human intellect (Manyika et al., 2017).

Another critical trend is the integration of AI with the Internet of Things (IoT). The fusion of AI and IoT, often referred to as AIoT, will facilitate more intelligent and responsive environments. From smart cities to intelligent manufacturing systems, AIoT will optimise resource utilisation, improve operational efficiency, and enhance user experiences by making real-time, data-driven decisions (Gandomi & Haider, 2015).

The rise of AI in cybersecurity is another area to watch. As cyber threats become more sophisticated, AI will play a crucial role in predicting, detecting, and mitigating these threats. Advanced machine learning models will analyse vast amounts of data to identify anomalies and potential security breaches, ensuring robust protection of critical assets (Mayer-Schönberger & Cukier, 2013).

Ethical AI and responsible AI practices are gaining traction. The focus is shifting towards ensuring that AI systems are transparent, fair, and accountable. This involves addressing biases in AI algorithms, protecting user privacy, and establishing clear governance frameworks. For instance, IBM's AI Fairness 360 toolkit provides resources to detect and mitigate bias in machine learning models, ensuring that AI decisions are more equitable and transparent (Bostrom, 2014).

The use of AI to enhance customer experiences is another burgeoning trend. Personalised AI-driven recommendations, chatbots, and virtual assistants are becoming more sophisticated, providing tailored and seamless interactions. Businesses leveraging these AI tools will be able to understand better and anticipate customer needs, leading to improved satisfaction and loyalty (Russell & Norvig, 2016).

The democratisation of AI technologies is making advanced tools and platforms accessible to a broader audience. Low-code and no-code AI development platforms enable individuals without deep technical expertise to build and deploy AI solutions. This will empower more professionals to innovate and integrate AI into their workflows, fostering a culture of continuous improvement and agility (Manyika et al., 2017).

Lastly, the convergence of AI with other emerging technologies, such as blockchain and quantum computing, will open new horizons. AI combined with blockchain can enhance transparency and security in transactions, while quantum computing will exponentially boost AI processing capabilities, solving problems that are currently intractable (Mayer-Schönberger & Cukier, 2013).

Conclusion

AI has the potential to revolutionise various aspects of life, from automating mundane tasks to solving complex global challenges. However, its development comes with significant ethical and practical considerations. As AI continues to evolve, it is crucial to ensure its fair and secure use while also preparing the workforce for new roles and responsibilities. Understanding and leveraging AI will be vital to staying competitive and innovative in the digital age. By addressing these challenges head-on and adopting a strategic approach to AI integration, businesses can harness the full potential of AI and drive meaningful innovation and growth.

References

- Bostrom, N. (2014). *Superintelligence: Paths, Dangers, Strategies.* Oxford University Press.
- Gandomi, A., & Haider, M. (2015). *Beyond the hype: Big data concepts, methods, and analytics.* International Journal of Information Management, 35(2), 137-144.
- Manyika, J., Chui, M., Brown, B., Bughin, J., Dobbs, R., Roxburgh, C., & Byers, A. H. (2017). *Big data: The next frontier for innovation, competition, and productivity.* McKinsey Global Institute.
- Mayer-Schönberger, V., & Cukier, K. (2013). *Big Data: A Revolution That Will*

Transform How We Live, Work, and Think. Houghton Mifflin Harcourt.
- Russell, S., & Norvig, P. (2016). *Artificial Intelligence: A Modern Approach*. Pearson.
- Russom, P. (2011). *Big data analytics*. TDWI Best Practices Report, Fourth Quarter, 19(4), 1-34.

Additional Reading

- Bessen, J. (2019). *AI and Jobs: The Role of Demand*. NBER Working Paper Series.
- Brynjolfsson, E., & McAfee, A. (2014). *The Second Machine Age: Work, Progress, and Prosperity in a Time of Brilliant Technologies*. W. W. Norton & Company.
- West, D. M. (2018). *The Future of Work: Robots, AI, and Automation*. Brookings Institution Press.

The Transformative Impact of Generative AI on Modern Business Operations

Abstract

Generative Artificial Intelligence (Gen AI) is revolutionising various industries by enabling machines to autonomously generate content and perform tasks that mimic human creativity and decision-making processes. This article explores the transformative potential of Gen AI across different domains, including healthcare, finance, design, and entertainment. It highlights the opportunities and challenges associated with integrating Gen AI into business operations, emphasising the importance of ethical considerations and continuous learning. By understanding and leveraging Gen AI, professionals can drive

innovation and achieve competitive advantages in the digital age.

Introduction

Generative AI represents a class of algorithms that allow machines to generate content autonomously, often mimicking human creativity and decision-making processes. Unlike traditional software that operates within predefined rules, Generative AI learns from vast amounts of data to produce outputs that can be remarkably nuanced and original. A prominent example of Generative AI is GPT-4, developed by OpenAI, which can generate human-like text based on the input it receives. This technology signifies a shift towards machines that perform tasks and exhibit a form of creativity previously thought to be exclusive to humans.

Exploring Generative AI and Its Potential

Generative AI holds transformative potential across various industries. In healthcare, algorithms like AlphaFold by DeepMind have revolutionised the prediction of protein structures, significantly advancing biomedical research (Senior et al., 2020). In finance, AI models can analyse market data to generate complex trading strategies in real time, adapting to dynamic market conditions faster than any human could (Manyika et al., 2017).

Moreover, in creative fields such as design and entertainment, Generative AI opens new frontiers. From generating new product designs based on user preferences to creating immersive virtual environments, the technology offers endless possibilities for innovation and customisation. For instance, companies like NVIDIA use Generative AI to create realistic graphics and virtual worlds for video games and simulations (Goodfellow et al., 2014).

Ethical and Practical Challenges

With these opportunities come challenges. Issues around ethical use, bias in data, and the potential misuse of AI-generated content need careful consideration. As experienced professionals, your insight into risk management and strategic foresight will be crucial in navigating these complexities. Ensuring transparency, accountability, and fairness in AI applications is essential to mitigate these risks (Bostrom & Yudkowsky, 2014).

Harnessing the Potential of Generative AI

To effectively harness the potential of Generative AI, organisations must invest in technology and build a culture that embraces experimentation and continuous learning. This involves fostering a mindset of innovation, upskilling employees, and integrating AI advancements into existing workflows. By doing so, businesses can achieve a competitive advantage in the digital age (Brynjolfsson & McAfee, 2014).

Case Studies

Walmart leverages big data and Generative AI to optimise its operations and enhance customer experiences. Processing over 2.5 petabytes of data every hour, Walmart uses AI to manage inventory, predict customer preferences, and personalise marketing efforts. This real-time data analysis allows Walmart to respond quickly to market changes, ensuring popular products are in stock and reducing waste from overstocking (Manyika et al., 2017).

Netflix employs Generative AI to recommend content to its users. By collecting data on viewing habits, search queries, and even the time of day users watch content, Netflix creates personalised recommendations, enhancing user experience and engagement.

This predictive analysis leads to higher satisfaction and retention rates, contributing significantly to Netflix's success (Gandomi & Haider, 2015).

Integrating Generative AI into Leadership and Management

Leadership today transcends traditional boundaries, harnessing data-driven insights and machine-learning algorithms to enhance decision-making processes. Generative AI has introduced adaptive leadership models that leverage technology to optimise efficiency and empower teams through real-time feedback and personalised development pathways. Tools like Microsoft Teams and Slack incorporate AI features to enhance team collaboration and provide instant feedback (Russell & Norvig, 2016).

The rise of AI-powered tools has democratised access to information, enabling leaders to gain deeper insights into market dynamics and consumer behaviours. This democratisation fosters inclusivity in decision-making processes, ensuring diverse perspectives are considered when shaping strategic initiatives (Bostrom, 2014).

Decision-Making in the Age of Generative AI

Imagine a future where decision-making boundaries are redrawn by algorithms capable of learning, reasoning, and generating insights autonomously. Generative AI, like OpenAI's GPT-4, empowers leaders to make more informed decisions swiftly, harnessing the collective intelligence embedded within data. This capability offers a strategic advantage by uncovering patterns and possibilities that human analysis might overlook (OpenAI, 2023).

Challenges in Integrating Generative AI

The journey towards integrating Generative AI into decision-making processes is not without challenges. From ethical considerations to operational readiness, navigating this landscape requires thoughtful consideration and proactive leadership. Addressing issues such as data privacy, algorithmic bias, and transparency is critical to maintaining stakeholder trust and ensuring responsible AI use (Mayer-Schönberger & Cukier, 2013).

Enhancing Creativity and Innovation

Generative AI can significantly amplify creativity and innovation. For example, in the automotive industry, companies like Tesla use AI to design more aerodynamic and efficient vehicles, pushing the boundaries of automotive design. In the retail sector, AI analyses vast datasets to predict trends with unprecedented accuracy, helping businesses tailor their offerings more precisely and meet consumer demands in real-time (Manyika et al., 2017).

Ethical and Societal Implications

Gen AI represents a significant leap forward in AI capabilities, but it also brings complex ethical considerations. Ensuring fairness and transparency in AI-driven decisions and addressing data privacy and security implications are critical. Current frameworks like the EU's General Data Protection Regulation (GDPR) and the proposed AI Act provide guidelines to ensure data privacy and security (European Commission, 2021).

Conclusion

Generative AI represents a paradigm shift in how we perceive machine capabilities. As seasoned professionals, understanding its implications will be pivotal in steering organisations towards future success. By embracing the potential of Generative AI while navigating its challenges, businesses can drive innovation, enhance decision-making, and achieve competitive advantages in the digital age.

References

- Bostrom, N., & Yudkowsky, E. (2014). *The ethics of artificial intelligence.* Cambridge Handbook of Artificial Intelligence, 316-334.
- Brynjolfsson, E., & McAfee, A. (2014). *The Second Machine Age: Work, Progress, and Prosperity in a Time of Brilliant Technologies.* W. W. Norton & Company.
- European Commission. (2021). *Proposal for a regulation laying down harmonised rules on artificial intelligence (Artificial Intelligence Act).*

Retrieved from <https://eur-lex.europa.eu/>
- Gandomi, A., & Haider, M. (2015). *Beyond the hype: Big data concepts, methods, and analytics.* International Journal of Information Management, 35(2), 137-144.
- Goodfellow, I., Pouget-Abadie, J., Mirza, M., Xu, B., Warde-Farley, D., Ozair, S., ... & Bengio, Y. (2014). Generative adversarial nets. In *Advances in neural information processing systems* (pp. 2672-2680).
- Manyika, J., Chui, M., Brown, B., Bughin, J., Dobbs, R., Roxburgh, C., & Byers, A. H. (2011). *Big data: The next frontier for innovation, competition, and productivity.* McKinsey Global Institute.
- Mayer-Schönberger, V., & Cukier, K. (2013). *Big Data: A Revolution That Will Transform How We Live, Work, and Think.* Houghton Mifflin Harcourt.
- OpenAI. (2023). *GPT-4 Technical Report.* Retrieved from <https://www.openai.com/research/>

- Russell, S., & Norvig, P. (2016). *Artificial Intelligence: A Modern Approach*. Pearson.
- Senior, A. W., Evans, R., Jumper, J., Kirkpatrick, J., Sifre, L., Green, T., ... & Hassabis, D. (2020). *Improved protein structure prediction using potentials from deep learning*. Nature, 577(7792), 706-710.

Additional Reading

- Bessen, J. (2019). *AI and Jobs: The Role of Demand*. NBER Working Paper Series.
- Tegmark, M. (2017). *Life 3.0: Being Human in the Age of Artificial Intelligence*. Knopf.

Cultivating an AI-Ready Organizational Culture

Abstract

In today's rapidly evolving business landscape, the influence of artificial intelligence (AI) is growing exponentially. To thrive in this environment, organisations must cultivate an AI-ready culture. This involves fostering continuous learning, promoting collaboration, ensuring ethical and transparent AI practices, and celebrating successes. By creating an AI-ready culture, businesses can harness AI's full potential, driving innovation and competitive advantage.

Introduction

The integration of AI into business operations is no longer a futuristic concept; it is a present necessity. To stay competitive, organisations must build an AI-ready culture. This culture emphasises continuous learning, cross-departmental collaboration, strong leadership support, and ethical considerations. This article explores how to cultivate such a culture and why it is essential for the success of modern businesses.

Commitment to Learning and Adaptability

Creating an AI-ready culture begins with a commitment to learning and adaptability. Continuous education and training for all employees are crucial. This helps everyone understand AI better and feel more comfortable using it. Encouraging a mindset where trying new things is valued, and failures are seen as learning opportunities fosters innovation and resilience.

For example, companies like Google and Amazon have implemented continuous learning programs to keep their workforce updated with the latest AI advancements. Google offers a variety of internal training programs and workshops on AI, allowing employees to stay abreast of new developments and integrate these advancements into their work processes (Spector, 2012).

Promoting a mindset of experimentation is also essential. Employees should feel encouraged to test new ideas and technologies without fear of failure. This approach accelerates learning and drives innovation by allowing employees to discover what works and what doesn't in real-time.

Promoting Teamwork and Collaboration

AI projects often require input from various departments, including IT, operations, marketing, and human resources. By breaking down silos and encouraging collaboration, organisations can leverage diverse perspectives and expertise, leading to more effective AI solutions. Promoting a culture of knowledge sharing, where

successes and insights are communicated across the organisation, is also vital.

For instance, Microsoft uses cross-functional teams to drive its AI initiatives, ensuring diverse expertise is leveraged for optimal results (Edmondson, 2012). These teams collaborate on projects from inception to deployment, bringing together a wide range of skills and knowledge to tackle complex AI challenges.

To facilitate collaboration, organisations can implement collaborative tools and platforms that enable seamless communication and teamwork. Platforms like Slack and Microsoft Teams, which include AI-driven features, can help enhance coordination and efficiency across different departments.

Leadership Support and Commitment

Leadership plays a crucial role in creating an AI-ready culture. Leaders must actively support AI initiatives and demonstrate their commitment through actions. This includes allocating resources for AI projects, celebrating AI successes, and addressing challenges openly. Leaders should also be open to learning about AI and its potential impact on their industry.

Satya Nadella, CEO of Microsoft, exemplifies a leader who champions AI, fostering a culture of innovation and continuous learning within the organisation (Nadella, 2017). Under his leadership, Microsoft has invested heavily in AI research and development, ensuring that the company stays at the forefront of technological advancements.

Leaders can also drive AI adoption by setting clear strategic goals for AI integration and aligning these goals with the organisation's overall vision and mission. This alignment helps ensure that AI initiatives receive the necessary support and resources to succeed.

Transparency and Ethical Considerations

AI can raise ethical issues, such as data privacy and bias. Establishing clear guidelines and ethical standards for AI use within the organisation is crucial. These standards should be communicated clearly and followed throughout the AI development and deployment processes. Encouraging open discussions about ethical issues and empowering employees to voice their concerns are also significant.

Frameworks like the EU's General Data Protection Regulation (GDPR) and the proposed AI Act provide guidelines to ensure data privacy and ethical AI use (Voigt & Bussche, 2017). Organisations should adopt these frameworks to guide their AI practices, ensuring compliance with legal standards and maintaining public trust.

Additionally, ethical AI practices should include regular audits and assessments to identify and mitigate potential biases in AI systems. Implementing fairness-aware algorithms and techniques such as SHAP (SHapley Additive exPlanations) and LIME (Local Interpretable Model-agnostic Explanations) can help in making AI decisions more transparent and equitable.

Fostering a Data-Driven Decision-Making Culture

AI relies on quality data to function effectively. Encouraging the collection, analysis, and use of data in decision-making processes is essential. Providing employees with the tools and skills they need to understand data insights improves decision-making accuracy and builds confidence in AI technologies.

Tools like Tableau and Power BI can help employees visualise and interpret data, making data-driven decisions more accessible (Chen et al., 2012). These tools allow employees to create interactive dashboards and reports that provide real-time insights into various business operations.

Organisations should also establish data governance policies to ensure data quality and integrity. This includes defining roles for data stewardship, setting data access protocols, and implementing data protection measures. Effective data governance enhances the reliability of AI models and protects against data breaches and misuse.

Recognising and Celebrating AI Successes

Highlighting successful AI projects and their impact on the organisation reinforces the value of AI and motivates further engagement. Creating platforms where employees can share their AI experiences and insights builds a community of AI advocates within the organisation.

IBM hosts internal AI innovation awards to celebrate and share successful AI projects across the company (Kelly & Hamm, 2013). These awards recognise teams and individuals who have made significant contributions to AI initiatives, encouraging a culture of innovation and excellence.

Regularly showcasing AI success stories through internal newsletters, webinars, and town hall meetings can also help build enthusiasm and support for AI initiatives. These platforms provide opportunities for employees to learn from each other and stay informed about the latest developments in AI.

Conclusion

Building an AI-ready organisational culture is not an overnight task, but with commitment and strategic action, it is achievable. By promoting learning, collaboration, ethical standards, data-driven decision-making, and celebrating successes, organisations can position themselves to thrive in an AI-driven future. Embracing these practices ensures that businesses are prepared to leverage AI's transformative power, driving innovation and maintaining a competitive edge.

References

- Chen, H., Chiang, R. H. L., & Storey, V. C. (2012). *Business Intelligence and Analytics: From Big Data to Big Impact*. MIS Quarterly, 36(4), 1165-1188.
- Edmondson, A. C. (2012). *Teaming: How Organizations Learn, Innovate, and Compete in the Knowledge Economy*. John Wiley & Sons.
- Kelly, J. E., & Hamm, S. (2013). *Smart Machines: IBM's Watson and the Era of Cognitive Computing*. Columbia University Press.
- Nadella, S. (2017). *Hit Refresh: The Quest to Rediscover Microsoft's Soul and Imagine a Better Future for Everyone*. Harper Business.
- Spector, B. (2012). *Implementing Organizational Change: Theory Into Practice*. Pearson.
- Voigt, P., & Bussche, A. V. D. (2017). *The EU General Data Protection Regulation (GDPR): A Practical Guide*. Springer.

Additional Reading

- Bostrom, N., & Yudkowsky, E. (2014). *The Ethics of Artificial Intelligence*. In K. Frankish & W. M. Ramsey (Eds.), The Cambridge Handbook of Artificial Intelligence. Cambridge University Press.
- Brynjolfsson, E., & McAfee, A. (2014). *The Second Machine Age: Work, Progress, and Prosperity in a Time of Brilliant Technologies*. W. W. Norton & Company.
- Davenport, T. H., & Kirby, J. (2016). *Only Humans Need Apply: Winners and Losers in the Age of Smart Machines*. Harper Business.
- West, D. M. (2018). *The Future of Work: Robots, AI, and Automation*. Brookings Institution Press.

About the Author

Partha Majumdar's leadership in the dynamic realm of software solutions is about technical prowess, strategic insight, and a unique style that blends these qualities with a personal touch. This makes his approach to innovation, efficiency, and business success unique.

His educational journey, which spans a Global Doctor of Business Administration to specialisations in Computational Data Sciences and Cybersecurity, reflects a commitment to continuous learning.

Majumdar's professional journey has been nothing short of extraordinary. As the Vice President of Software Engineering at J.P. Morgan Chase and Co. in his last role, he has spearheaded impactful initiatives, contributing to the evolution of software development paradigms. He is in the inception phase of starting his firm in the UAE and pursuing his PhD in Computer Science from Kalinga University. His earlier role as the Managing Director of Majumdar Consultancy Private Limited showcased his entrepreneurial spirit, where he successfully nurtured a fledgling business into a success with a global footprint.

Partha Majumdar's diverse talents and expertise are not confined to a single domain. His proficiency in software development, predictive modelling, descriptive data analysis, and Agile Project Management is a testament to his versatility, adaptability, and ability to deliver innovative solutions across various contexts.

Beyond his roles in corporate leadership, Majumdar has been recognised with numerous awards, including the "Excellence Award," "Gratitude Award," "Merit Award," and "Best IT Manager," underscoring his impact and leadership in the field. His commitment to excellence is further demonstrated through a comprehensive list of professional upskilling, covering project management, IT service management, and specialised areas like data science and cloud computing.

Majumdar's publications and patent attempts showcase a commitment to advancing the field. He has published twenty-one books on academia and knowledge dissemination, and his upcoming books and publications illustrate his dedication to sharing knowledge and insights.

In conclusion, Partha Majumdar's career is a testament to his multifaceted expertise, from spearheading successful ventures to influencing software development paradigms at industry giants. His unwavering commitment to innovation, coupled with a rich educational background and many certificates, positions him as a distinguished leader poised to continue making impactful contributions in the ever-evolving landscape of software solutions.

Books by the Author

Mastering Classification Algorithms for Machine Learning

This book delves into the core of machine learning through the lens of classification algorithms, which play a pivotal role in categorising input based on its features. These algorithms are the backbone of various applications, from spam detection to fraud prevention. Starting with a foundational overview of problem-solving in machine learning, the book transitions to a focused examination of classification challenges. It provides an in-depth exploration of the Naïve Bayes algorithm, Logistic Regression, including the crucial sigmoid function, and Decision Trees, highlighting critical concepts like the Gini Factor and Entropy. Furthermore, it elaborates on the Random Forest algorithm and concludes with an insightful discussion on Boosting techniques, offering a comprehensive guide to mastering classification algorithms in machine learning.

Link In Amazon Store:
https://www.amazon.com/dp/935551851X

Machine Learning for Managers

This book is a comprehensive guide tailored for leaders aiming to leverage machine learning (ML) within their organisations. It simplifies ML concepts, emphasising strategic applications over technical complexity. The book covers integrating ML into business practices, ethical data use, and real-world industry applications, showcasing ML's role in enhancing operations and innovation. It also provides insights on team building in the ML era, promoting cross-disciplinary collaboration for effective ML adoption. This book is a strategic roadmap for managers to harness ML, driving informed decision-making and positioning their organisations for future success in an AI-driven landscape.

Link in Amazon Store: https://www.amazon.in/dp/B0CZ5XTQ1L

Deep Learning for Managers

This book is a pivotal guide for modern leaders navigating the AI revolution. It demystifies deep learning, making it accessible to managers without requiring deep technical knowledge. This book equips leaders with the insights to harness AI effectively, covering everything from the basics of artificial neural networks to the ethical considerations of AI deployment. It's an indispensable resource for any leader aiming to leverage deep learning as a strategic asset in today's rapidly evolving business landscape.

Link in Amazon Store: https://www.amazon.in/dp/B0CWDPWSN8

Generative AI for Managers

This book is a cutting-edge guide that demystifies Generative AI for business leaders eager to harness this technology for growth and innovation. It delves into how Generative AI can revolutionise aspects of business, from enhancing customer experiences to optimising operations and driving strategic decision-making. The book provides a wealth of practical applications, showcases how mundane tasks can be automated for efficiency, and presents strategies for fostering a culture of innovation through AI. Additionally, it offers guidance on the ethical implementation of AI technologies, ensuring they complement and augment human capabilities within the organisational framework, thereby paving the way for a future rich in opportunities and advancements.

Link in Amazon Store: https://www.amazon.in/dp/B0CXYBFJHD

ChatGPT AI for Managers

This book is a vital resource for leaders navigating the AI revolution, focusing on integrating Generative AI, like ChatGPT, in enhancing managerial functions and team dynamics. It provides practical insights into leveraging ChatGPT to streamline tasks, bolster decision-making, and encourage innovative thinking within teams. This guide transcends theoretical knowledge, offering actionable strategies for managers to complement their skills with AI, thereby elevating their leadership effectiveness. Through real-world applications and expert advice, readers will learn to harmonise traditional management with AI advancements, ensuring they remain at the forefront of the evolving business environment.

Link in Amazon Store: https://www.amazon.in/dp/B0CY8L4CQ9

Data Lakes for Managers

This book is a guide tailored for managers, detailing how to utilise data lakes effectively. It simplifies complex concepts and focuses on practical strategies and the strategic use of data lake technologies like AWS, Azure, and GCP. The book addresses common challenges such as data silos and security. It offers insights into the future of data technologies, empowering managers to harness data for strategic decision-making and innovation.

Link in Amazon Store:
https://www.amazon.in/dp/B0D35RCDPD

Recommendation Systems for Managers

This book demystifies the complexities of data-driven recommendation systems in an easy-to-understand format tailored for managers. This insightful guide traverses Time Series and Market Basket Analysis, AI, ML, and emerging technologies, offering a practical roadmap for implementing these systems. It's an indispensable resource for managers aiming to harness recommendation systems for strategic business decisions in the digital age.

Link in Amazon Store:
https://www.amazon.in/dp/B0CXNNSJRC

Learn Emotion Analysis with R

This book is a comprehensive guide to Emotion Analysis using Lexicons, offering a step-by-step code walkthrough for developing Sentiment and Emotion Analysis systems with data from WhatsApp and Twitter. It introduces R and Shiny programming, which is essential for building emotion analysis systems. The discussion then extends to the fundamentals of Sentiment and Emotion Analysis, leading to the creation of Shiny applications tailored for this purpose. The book concludes by developing a specialised tool for analysing emotions from Twitter and WhatsApp data. Additionally, it hints at advancing into Machine Learning for Emotion Analysis, contingent on the availability of labelled data, positioning this as a subsequent step for readers.

Link in Amazon Store: https://www.amazon.com/dp/B096K2SVF2

Linear Programming for Project Management Professionals

This guide provides project management professionals with strategies for project crashing using linear programming, ensuring timely completion and cost efficiency. It introduces basic project management concepts, monitoring techniques, and linear programming problem formulation. The book explains how to solve these problems using Microsoft Excel's Solver and applying time and cost optimisation methods to real-world scenarios. It equips project management teams with a comprehensive toolkit to handle complex challenges effectively.

Link in Amazon Store: https://www.amazon.com/dp/B09PD1GFMY

Gartner Research Analysis

The book provides a clear framework for leveraging insights from the Gartner Hype-Cycle Report, an essential resource for understanding technological trends. It simplifies identifying and evaluating emerging technologies, their developers, and market readiness. A live case study illustrates practical application while emphasising the need for comprehensive research beyond the report. Essential for those seeking strategic technological guidance, this book demystifies the complex data presented in the Gartner Hype Cycle.

Link in Amazon Store: https://www.amazon.com/dp/B0CK582Y2M

Starting a New AI Business

This book is a comprehensive guide designed for entrepreneurs looking to harness the power of artificial intelligence to build successful enterprises. Covering everything from defining business purpose and understanding AI fundamentals to exploring innovative business models and identifying market opportunities, this book provides practical insights and strategic guidance. With case studies of industry giants and lessons from ancient wisdom, it equips readers with the tools and knowledge to navigate the AI landscape effectively and achieve sustainable growth.

Link in Amazon Store: https://www.amazon.in/dp/B0CL3YBSF8

Corporate Lessons I Learned

This book encapsulates 34 years of corporate experiences up to 2023, presenting a collection of impactful incidents and interactions that shaped the author's career. Primarily aimed at middle and lower-level managers, it offers humorous and insightful recollections that serve as practical guidelines for navigating daily challenges in the corporate world. The author illustrates valuable lessons learned through various encounters, making it a helpful resource for understanding and excelling in corporate management.

Link in Amazon Store: https://www.amazon.in/dp/B0CL3YBSF8

Mutual Fund Investing

This book is a comprehensive guide for middle-class investors in India, simplifying mutual funds. It covers types of mutual funds, differences between open-ended and closed funds, systematic investments, tax implications, and risk assessment. It also teaches advanced techniques like Piotrowski's F-Score and Mohanram's G-Score for building diversified portfolios and evaluating fund performance. Suitable for beginners and seasoned investors, it is essential for achieving financial growth and security through mutual funds.

Link in Amazon Store: https://www.amazon.com/dp/B0CYNG6B12

Creating an Investment Portfolio

This book delves into the scientific process of making informed investment decisions, highlighting the importance for individuals and corporations. It explores critical theories and applications in portfolio creation, covering various investment vehicles like fixed deposits, mutual funds, and shares, emphasising the necessary mathematics. Additionally, it introduces simple yet widely used tools for investment calculations. Designed to be accessible to a broad audience, this book is an invaluable guide for beginners and experienced investors aiming to enhance their understanding and effectiveness in investing.

Link in Amazon Store: https://www.amazon.com/dp/B0CK99SPKZ

Essay on the Indian Knowledge System – Part 1

The book delves into the Indian Knowledge System (IKS), a comprehensive approach to compiling, conserving, and disseminating India's rich knowledge heritage across various disciplines such as science, mathematics, social sciences, medicine, philosophy, art, and spirituality. It highlights the global perspective of IKS and its relevance in sharing India's intellectual legacy with the world. The study of Indology, or "Bharatatattva," as it's known in Indian scholarship, further explores the historical, cultural, linguistic, and literary facets of the Indian subcontinent. Through a series of concise essays, this book, one of a trilogy on ancient India, offers insights into Bharatatattva, underscoring India's significant contributions to global knowledge.

Link in Amazon Store: https://www.amazon.com/dp/B0CXNN95TR

Good People Are Tested the Most

This book explores the lives of seven extraordinary individuals who faced immense challenges and emerged victorious. The book delves into resilience, faith, and the triumph of the human spirit, featuring Bhakt Prahalad, Raja Harishchandra, Lord Shri Ram, Arjun, Hercules, Swami Vivekananda, and Sardar Milkha Singh. Their inspiring stories highlight the importance of maintaining principles, overcoming significant challenges, and the ultimate triumph of good over evil, serving as inspiration for all.

Link in Amazon Store: https://www.amazon.in/dp/B0D1FM44H9

Sailing through the Kali Yug

This book explores the relevance of ancient Indian scriptures, especially the Purans, in understanding the complexities of the present age. It introduces the concept of Yugs, highlighting Rishi Krishna Dwaipayan Ved Vyas's role and the Purans' structure. The book details the moral decline of the Kali Yug, starting from Raja Parikshit's reign, and emphasises Dharam's four pillars. It promotes Bhakti and practical spiritual practices as pathways to maintaining integrity and achieving liberation.

Link in Amazon Store:
https://www.amazon.in/dp/B0D6M34JCT

The Maha Purans in Brief

This book distils the essence of eighteen ancient Vedic scriptures, offering insights into their themes, stories, and teachings. The book explores the relevance of Puranic wisdom in modern life, providing guidance on ethics, leadership, environmental sustainability, and personal development. It serves as an accessible guide to understanding the rich spiritual heritage of Indian culture and applying its timeless lessons to contemporary challenges.

Link in Amazon Store:
https://www.amazon.in/dp/B0CW8GJ22L

Weekend in Jordan

Thanks to the country's visa-on-arrival policy for Indians, the authors spontaneously travelled to Jordan to celebrate their 20th wedding anniversary. Their weekend was filled with memorable experiences, from Petra's historical wonders to the Dead Sea's unique allure and Amman's vibrant city life. Despite its modest size, Jordan's rich offerings left a lasting impression. This book recounts their remarkable journey, providing insights into the treasures of Jordan.

Link in Amazon Store: https://www.amazon.com/dp/B0CK5N6B3W

Elephant Ride in Chang Wangpo

In 2022, Thailand saw a significant influx of approximately 11.5 million tourists, underlining tourism's vital role in its economy, contributing around 6% to the Thai GDP. Reflecting on their past residency in Bangkok from 1996 to 1999, the authors seized a chance to revisit Thailand in 2018, noticing considerable changes. An efficient metro system has alleviated the once notorious Bangkok traffic, enhancing city navigation. While many cherished aspects remained, improvements in the road network and increased attractions enriched their experience. Coinciding with their 26th wedding anniversary, the business trip also included leisure exploration in Bangkok and Kanchanaburi, with a memorable visit to Chang Wangpo, blending nostalgia, discovery, and celebration.

Link in Amazon Store: https://www.amazon.com/dp/B0CKGWH97S

Weekend in South Sikkim

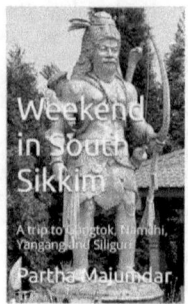

This book explores the less-travelled South Sikkim, diverging from popular tourist spots like Gangtok and Nathu La Pass. It covers captivating destinations such as Tsomgo Lake, Baba Ka Mandir, and Temi Tea Gardens. The authors delve into the cultural and spiritual essence of South Sikkim with visits to Namchi's Char Dham and Samdruptse Monastery. The narrative also extends to Yangang and the Bengal Safari in Siliguri, West Bengal, offering a comprehensive travelogue with diverse experiences.

Link in Amazon Store:
https://www.amazon.com/dp/B0CKL1DNTJ

Trips to Dubai

This travelogue unveils the multifaceted allure of Dubai, a top-tier tourist hub known for landmarks like the Burj Khalifa and Burj Al Arab, alongside thrilling experiences such as helicopter rides and dolphin encounters at the Atlantis. It extends beyond Dubai, shedding light on Abu Dhabi and Sharjah attractions, like the adrenaline-pumping Ferrari World and the enchanting Desert Safari. The author shares personal adventures, offering insights into the intricacies of visiting Dubai and navigating the Gulf region, making this book a valuable resource for anyone looking to explore the rich experiences Dubai and its neighbouring emirates offer.

Link in Amazon Store: https://www.amazon.com/dp/B0CKRYQKDN

1-Day Trips from Bengaluru

From 1975 to 2023, Bengaluru evolved from a retirees' haven to India's Silicon Valley, also renowned as Garden City. While Bengaluru has numerous tourist attractions and activity hubs, the city's vicinity offers many exploration destinations. This book focuses on day-trip-worthy spots around Bengaluru, places steeped in historical and mythological significance. It does not cover prominent cities like Mysuru, Chennai, and Hyderabad, as well as scenic locales like Ooty, Goa, and Kerala, as they need more than a day to tour.

Link in Amazon Store: https://www.amazon.com/dp/B0CLK58KTB

A Trip to the Wagah Border

The Wagah Border, straddling India and Pakistan near Amritsar and Lahore, is famed for its ceremonial displays by border forces, symbolising hope amidst strained relations. This checkpoint, pivotal for prisoner exchanges, represents a unique reconciliation potential. On festive occasions, friendly exchanges between the forces foster harmony. The book visually explores Chandigarh, Shimla, Amritsar, and the Wagah Border, highlighting their rich cultures and historical importance.

Link in Amazon Store: https://www.amazon.com/dp/B0CLYTQ6PV

Weekend Getaways from Bengaluru

This guidebook enhances the tourism experience in India, emphasising the country's improved accessibility and facilities that cater to all traveller categories. It explicitly outlines short trips from Bengaluru, covering a mix of destinations accessible by road, rail, and air. The book is a resource for planning 2-, 3-, and 4-day excursions to various South Indian locales and select sites in Maharashtra, featuring popular tourist destinations such as Ooty, Kodaikanal, and Mysuru, as well as revered places of worship like Kukke Subramanya and Dharamsthala. It offers practical travel tips, what to anticipate on journeys and insights into each destination's unique offerings.

Link in Amazon Store: https://www.amazon.com/dp/B0CMNRKWQ9

www.ingramcontent.com/pod-product-compliance
Lightning Source LLC
Chambersburg PA
CBHW071918210526
45479CB00002B/463